CHILD PHONOLOGY
A Book of Exercises for Students

Ken M. Bleile, Ph.D.

SINGULAR PUBLISHING GROUP, INC.
SAN DIEGO, CALIFORNIA

Singular Publishing Group, Inc.
4284 41st Street
San Diego, California 92105

ISBN 1-879105-31-4

Printed in the United States of America

For Terry Helinski

CONTENTS

PREFACE

This book is based on the premise that one of the best ways to learn child phonology is to learn to solve phonological problems. Working on phonological problems helps students develop the analytical skills necessary to use phonological data creatively, whether for purposes of research or for developing clinical evaluation and therapy programs for clients with communication disorders. Relatedly, learning how to solve phonological problems often helps students develop a deeper comprehension of the phonological studies that they read as part of their class work and that many will continue to read throughout their professional lives.

This book is intended primarily for students in graduate and advanced undergraduate courses on articulatory and phonological disorders. Sections of the book are also appropriate for courses in psycholinguistics, language acquisition, phonology, and introductory courses in speech-language pathology. The conceptual and theoretical underpinnings of the exercises are sufficiently broad that the book can be used in conjunction with any number of different textbooks and by instructors from a wide variety of theoretical backgrounds.

Child Phonology has undergone extensive field testing. The book was originally developed for classes and seminars on phonology at the University of Iowa. Subsequently, while continuing to be used at the University of Iowa, the book was also field tested in courses at the University of Nebraska, Purdue University, and Memphis State University. Student and instructor comments have been quite favorable.

Child Phonology is organized into three main sections. The Introduction is a review of preliminaries to performing phonological analyses. These preliminaries include discussion of basic terminology and concepts in phonetics and phonology. Section I is devoted to normal development. Chapters in this section focus on restrictions on children's phonologies, the relationship between children's speech and the adult language, phonological systems undergoing change, and individual differences. Section II contains chapters on the assessment and remediation of clients with communication disorders. The book concludes with an appendix that provides suggested answers to the exercises.

ACKNOWLEDGMENTS

It is a pleasure to acknowledge those who assisted in the development of this book. My first thanks go to my teachers at the University of Oregon and the University of Iowa, whose influence is reflected in many of these pages. I especially wish to thank Bruce Tomblin, who, as both my academic and dissertation advisor at the University of Iowa, provided me a model as a teacher and colleague.

This book benefitted from the input of many individuals. I want to thank the many students I have had the pleasure to teach over the years, especially those who suffered through earlier versions of this book. I also want to thank John Bernthal, Karen Pollack, Richard Schwartz, and Amy Weiss, who paid me the courtesy of field testing this book.

Based on reader feedback, this book underwent extensive revisions. I wish to express my gratitude to Children's Seashore House for providing me the time and encouragement to complete the project. I also wish to thank the Department of Otorhinolaryngology and Human Communication for providing the laboratory space in which the majority of work on this book was undertaken.

Lastly, I wish to thank those involved in the book's publication, including John Bernthal, who encouraged me to submit the manuscript to Singular Publishing Group; Joy McGowan, who provided expert assistance in the preparation of the final manuscript; and the publisher and editors at Singular Publishing Group, who made the publication process so pleasurable.

INTRODUCTION

Review of Basic Concepts and Terminology

Speech-language pathologists are mainly interested in child phonology due to the insights it can provide into the evaluation and treatment of individuals with communication difficulties. Since the mid-1970s, when the impact of child phonology began to emerge in speech-language pathology, child phonology in its many schools of thought has provided the basis for numerous studies of communication disorders. A selection of those studies is represented in this book.

All academic disciplines, child phonology included, contain areas of controversy. Current "hot topics" in child phonology include the relationship between phonology and speech motor control (Folkins & Bleile, 1990; Shriberg & Widder, 1990), the psychological reality of phonological processes (McReynolds & Elbert, 1984), and the nature of phonological knowledge (Elbert, Dinnsen, & Weismer, 1984). This book is not the forum in which to resolve these issues. Instead, where possible, the book focuses on the types of phonological analyses that the majority of phonologists would most likely agree are important to know.

Terminology and notation themselves are matters of controversy in child phonology, however, and these issues cannot be wholly avoided, because a common terminology and notational system is needed before beginning the problems in the next section. For this reason, this chapter is devoted to defining selected terminology and notational conventions. These definitions will not satisfy all readers, nor are they necessary assumptions to undertaking the exercises. Offering these definitions may, however, reduce the confusion of students who perform these exercises by making the biases of the book more apparent. The assumption in the discussion that follows is that the reader is familiar with much of the material, so that the presentation is more of a review than an introduction to new ideas.

Child phonology is defined in this book as the study of the organization of sound by children acquiring their native language. This definition excludes second-language acquisition and non-oral languages, such as American Sign Language. This is a questionable distinction in theory, but it fits the present practical purposes. Due to the perceived nature of the audience and the nature of the existing data sources, consideration of child phonology is further restricted chiefly to English in the domains of words, stress, syllables, segments, and distinctive features. Intonation and phonological perception, though important topics in their own right, are not treated here. Lastly, none of the exercises in the book attempts to distinguish between phonology and speech motor control.

The term phonological process is avoided throughout the book. This term has different meanings to different users, and its inclusion would more likely confuse than help readers. Instead, the neutral term phonological pattern is employed (Bleile, 1989).

Phonological patterns are intended as descriptions of differences between the adult language and the child's speech. The term is descriptive in nature, and no claims are made regarding the nature of the psychological reality underlying the construct.

Syllables are given "flat" structures in the present book (Clements & Keyser, 1985). For example, the word "lips" has the following syllable structure:

This is not the only structure this syllable might have. For example, in some approaches the syllable might be organized hierarchically (Selkirk, 1984). One hierarchial unit often proposed in these approaches is the rime.

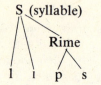

The author has not found a hierarchical syllable structure to be particularly helpful in understanding the phonologies of clients with communication disorders; however, any of the exercises in the book could be undertaken using this approach.

Phonotactics is an important concept in many of the exercises that follow. **Phonotactics** refers to the sequential arrangement of phonological units. For example, the phonotactics of English permits words to begin with consonant clusters such as [st], but disallows word-initial consonant clusters such as [ld].

Closely related to phonotactics are the concepts of occurrence restrictions and co-occurrence restrictions. **Occurrence restrictions** specify the phonetic environments in which a phonological unit can occur. To illustrate, a common occurrence restriction in children's phonologies is that voiced oral stops occur in word-initial position. **Co-occurrence restrictions** specify which combinations of units are permitted by the phonology. Co-occurrence restrictions motivate many patterns found in children's phonologies. For example, a common co-occurrence restriction in the phonologies of many young children is that both consonants in a word must be made at the same place of articulation. This co-occurrence restriction can motivate the pronunciation of words such as "take" [teɪk] as [keɪk].

The consonants and vowels of English appear in Tables 1–1 and 1–2, respectively. The tables appear to give articulatory definitions of speech sounds. For example, [t] is defined as alveolar, voiceless, and stop. However, these articulatory definitions should be considered with caution, because a sound perceived as [t] can actually be produced in a variety of ways. For example, [t] can be made with the tongue tip behind either the two upper front teeth or the two lower front teeth. For this reason, speech sounds might be considered units of perception rather than instructions to articulators.

Phonologists use a number of different distinctive feature systems to classify the speech sounds of English. Selection of a feature system can have an important influence on phonological analysis. To illustrate, at least one feature system classifies velar and labial sounds together (Jakobson & Halle, 1956), which permits certain sound changes to be readily explained, whereas another system classifies labial and alveolar sounds together (Chomsky & Halle, 1968), which permits other sound changes to be described. Selection of a feature system is not arbitrary, but, like all other choices in phonological analysis, is the result of theoretical decisions.

Table 1–1. The Consonants of English

Manner	Place							
	Bilabial	Labiodental	Interdental	Alveolar	Palato-Alveolar	Palatal	Velar	Glottal
Stop								
voiceless	p			t			k	
voiced	b			d				
Affricate								
voiceless					tʃ			
voiced					dʒ			
Fricative								
voiceless		f	θ	s	ʃ			h
voiced		v	ð	z	ʒ			
Nasal	m			n			ŋ	
Lateral Approximant				l				
Central Approximant				r		j	w	w

Table 1-2. English Vowels and Dipthongs

Height	Front		Central		Back	
	Tense	Lax	Tense	Lax	Tense	Lax
High	i	ɪ			u	ʊ
Mid	eɪ	ɛ		ɝ	oʊ	
				ʌ ə	ɔ	
					ɔɪ	
Low		æ	a		ɑ	
			aɪ			
			aʊ			

The exercises in this book do not depend on the use of any specific distinctive feature system. One possibility, though not necessarily the one recommended, is to use the consonant and vowel charts in Tables 1-1 and 1-2 as simple feature systems. For example, using these charts, [b] has the features of voice, bilabial, and stop. Similarly, [i] has the features of high, front, and tense. Readers who want the greater analytical power afforded by more formal feature systems might explore using those of Chomsky and Halle (1968), Ladefoged (1984), or Stoel-Gammon and Dunn (1985).

In addition to knowledge of consonants, vowels, and distinctive features, a number of problems in the text require the ability to read and use diacritics. **Diacritics** specify phonetic details of consonants and vowels. In some cases, diacritics provide important information regarding the child's phonology. Table 1-3 lists the diacritics used in this book.

Finally, the concept of levels of organization functions as a useful descriptive tool in this book. **Levels of organization** specify the phonological units that combine to form words or phrases. Throughout this book, possible levels of organization include word, stress, syllable, segment, and distinctive features, occurrence and co-occurrence restrictions. To illustrate, below are the levels of organization of the word "pigtail."

Word	pigtail					
Syllable Shape(s)	CVC.CVC					
Primary Stress	first syllable					
Syllable Type(s)	CVC					
Segments	p	ɪ	g	t	eɪ	l
Distinctive Features	bilabial	front	velar	alveolar	front	lateral
	stop	high	stop	stop	mid	
	-voice	lax	+voice	-voice	tense	

If there were occurrence or co-occurrence restrictions in the word, they would be described in prose on a line below the distinctive features. To illustrate, a phonology in which all consonants in words need to agree in place of articulation would contain a statement such as, "Consonants in words need to agree in place of articulation."

Table 1–3. Diacritics

Description	Symbol	Example	
aspiration	[Cʰ]	pit	[pʰɪt]
devoiced	[Ç]	bud	[bʌd̥]
lip rounding	[Cʷ]	two	[t̬u]
syllabic consonant	[Ç]	battle	[bæɫl̩]
velarization	[ɛ]	call	[kɔɫ]
flapping	[ɾ]	butter	[bʌɾə]
dentalization	[Ç]	tenth	[tɛn̪θ]

Readers familiar with linguistics will recognize that the concept of levels of organization is clearly related to the concept of "tiers" in Autosegmental Phonology (Goldsmith, 1976, 1990). After considerable thought, it was decided to use the term levels of organization instead of tiers because this book does not purport to be a primer on Autosegmental Phonology, and it was felt that using a term from Autosegmental Phonology might give the false impression that performing the exercises in this book constitutes experience in analyzing phonology from an Autosegmental perspective.

In addition to the definitions just discussed, a number of other definitions and notational devices are needed to solve the problems that follow. These are:

sibilant	Alveolar and palato-alveolar fricatives and affricates
obstruent	Oral stops, fricatives, and affricates
approximant	Glides and liquids
homeorganic	Sounds produced at the same place of articulation
labial	Bilabial and labio-dental consonants
apical	Sounds made with the tongue tip
CV	Consonant, vowel
segment	What is often called a speech sound, sound, phone, or phoneme. In this book the terms segment, phone, and speech sound are used interchangeably. The term phoneme is reserved to refer to functional oppositions in children's phonology.
resyllabification	Movement of a segment from its original syllable. To illustrate, word-final consonants are often resyllabified when the following word begins with a vowel. Resyllabification yields pronunciations such as [ɪ tɪz] for "it is."
[ ]	Phonetic transcription
/ /	Phonemic transcription. For the sake of readability, words within phonetic brackets and phonemic slashes are separated. For example, "big house" would be transcribed phonemically as /bɪg haʊs/.

assimiliation	The influence of one sound on another. For example, in "please" the [l] is often voiceless or partially voiced due to the influence of [p]. Assimilation that is caused by the influence of an earlier sound (as in "please") is called *preservatory assimilation*. Assimilation that results from the influence of a later sound is called *anticipatory assimilation*. To illustrate, [n] is often produced as a dental consonant in words ending in a dental consonant, such as "tenth."
A/B	The slash indicates an alternation. For example, if a child alternated between [p] and [b] in saying "bee," then the alternation would be signified as p/b.
optional	Alternations in production of a sound or sounds in a word
exceptions	Words that fail to follow general rules
X;Y:Z	Years;months:days. For example, a child 1 year, 6 months, 7 days old would be 1;6:7.
.	Syllable boundary (example: "about" [ə.baʊt]). The dot is used principally when a sequence of vowels could be interpreted as a diphthong or two separate vowels.
'	Primary stress (example: money [mʌ'ni]). Stress in the child's words is not marked unless it differs from that in adult English.
[ɲ] or /ɲ/	Palatal nasal
[x] or /x/	Voiceless velar fricative
+	In this book, when a plus appears before a child's pronunciation, it means the production was derived from a pattern described in an analysis in the literature, but that the actual pronunciation was not given in the source. For example, an analysis might have described a pattern in which a child said [p] for adult-language [t], but gave no examples. For an assignment based on this pattern, an additional example of the pattern might be created (e.g., [poʊ] for [toʊ]).

Review Exercises

Exercise 1

This problem focuses on definitions of basic terminology in phonetics and phonology. Answers to the problems appear at the end of the book.

1.1 Which consonants are nasal?

1.2 Which sound classes are obstruents?

1.3 Which classes of consonants are labials?

1.4 Which vowels are front?

1.5 Which vowels are high?

1.6 How many syllables does the following nonsense word have, [yi.oʊts.a.baˈɪ.ʊ]? Which syllable has primary stress?

1.7 What is meant when segments are put between slashes?
What is meant when segments are put between brackets?

1.8 Use features to describe the following sets of sounds.

    a. d g

    b. i u

    c. l r

    d. l r j w

    e. i eɪ

    f. eɪɛ

    g. s

1.9 What is assimilation?
What is anticipatory assimilation?
What is preservatory assimilation?

An important aspect of phonology is learning to use knowledge of phonetics creatively. Use your knowledge of phonetics to explain the following patterns.

1.10 Why is [t] usually a dental consonant in the word "tenth?"
(*Hint:* This question and those that follow are asking you both to identify the type of assimilation involved and to provide a reasonable phonetic explanation for why the assimilation occurred.)

1.11 Why is [r] usually voiceless in the word "pride"?

1.12 In your own words, explain why "Chomsky" is often pronounced with a [p] between [m] and [s].

Exercise 2

The next three problems offer opportunities to brush up on rusty transcription skills. All three exercises focus on transcription of either careful or casual speech. The difference between these two styles of speech can be surprisingly large. Perhaps the most often cited example of this difference is the phrase, "Did you eat yet?" In careful speech this might be pronounced [dɪd yu it yɛt], and in very casual speech it could be pronounced [dʒit dʒɛt].

Transcribe each of the following words as you would say them carefully in isolation, or, better yet, have someone say them carefully and slowly, and transcribe that person's speech. Use diacritics to indicate aspiration, devoicing of consonants in clusters, and lip rounding.

2.1   cat

2.2   thin

2.3   unite

2.4   brew

2.5   giving

2.6   fingernail polish

2.7   century

2.8 please

2.9 winter

2.10 between

Exercise 3

This exercise focuses on the transcription of casual speech. Transcribe the following words and phrases as if they were spoken in casual conversation, or have someone say them and transcribe that person's speech. Use all the diacritics in the previous assignment, plus the symbols for syllabic consonants and velarization.

3.1 button

3.2 university

3.3 single person

3.4 bottle

3.5 bacon and eggs

3.6 Did you go?

3.7 city

3.8 spangle

3.9 sound and fury

3.10 Where you going?

Exercise 4

This problem provides practice in transcribing both careful and casual speech. Indicate the syllables, consonants, and vowels in the following transcriptions. Use S for syllable, C for consonant, and V for vowel. To illustrate, "Tom is able" might have the following syllable shapes in extremely careful and casual speech:

	Careful	*Casual*
Tom is able	tɑmɪzeɪbʊl	tɑmɪzeɪbl̩

In the above example, the changes in syllable structure occur in "able" ([bʊl] becomes [bl̩]) and "Tom is" [tɑ mɪz] becomes [tɑm ɪz]). Both changes are the result of regular phonological rules of English.

		Careful	*Casual*
4.1	possible	pɑsɪbʊl	pɑsɪbl̩
4.2	it is	ɪtɪz	ɪtɪz

		Careful	*Casual*
4.3	button	bʌtɪn	bʌʔn
4.4	time and money	taɪmændmʌni	taɪmŋmʌni
4.5	this old man	ðɪsouldmæn	ðɪsouldmæn

SECTION I

Normal Development

The chapters in this section address a variety of issues related to phonological development. Topics include an introduction to two basic analytical procedures and studies of phonological change and individual differences. All the assignments in this section contain data from children without phonological disabilities. Phonological development in children without delays is a fascinating branch of study in its own right, and, of course, an understanding of what is normal and expected is a prerequisite to understanding what might be abnormal and disordered.

All the exercises present data from individual children. To help place these data in a wider perspective, however, the following discussion describes selected major milestones in the acquisition of English phonology. The information for this discussion comes from various sources, including descriptive studies, clinical assessment instruments, and, occasionally, professional experience. The ages given for the milestones are intended as approximations of the age range over which the acquisition of phonology occurs.

Table 2–1 summarizes selected early milestones in phonological development. Milestones in phonetic inventories are presented for children from birth to 3 years. Milestones in the development of intonation, communication, speech play, and imitation are presented for children from birth to 2 years.

As Table 2–1 indicates, the acquisition of phonology is often considered to begin early in the first year of life. Activities performed during this period permit the child to explore his speech capacities and to practice control of his articulators (Locke, 1983, 1986; Oller, 1980; Stark, 1980). The earliest precursors to speech are vegetative sounds produced during the first month of life. Cooing begins in the second and third months. Sounds produced during this period are generally made in the back of the mouth, perhaps reflecting patterns of myelination in the brain (Salus & Salus, 1974).

Near 3 and 4 months of age, children begin babbling consonant- and vowel-like sounds. At approximately the same time, they begin producing more sounds in the front of the mouth, including squeals, growls, raspberries, and trills. Babbling continues to evolve until the seventh or eighth month, when children's babbling comes to consist of repetitions of the same consonants and vowels, such as [ba ba ba] or [di di]. A few months later, at approximately 10 months of age, babbling evolves into combinations of consonant- and vowel-like sounds, such as [bi da bu].

At approximately 10 months, children begin using words. By 15 months, children's speech consists primarily of stops and nasals. Syllables consist of simple alternations of consonants and vowels. By approximately 24 months, children have 9 to 10 consonants in word-initial position and 5 to 6 consonants in word-final position. Most commonly, word-initial consonants are stops, nasals, glides, and the voiceless fricatives [f s]. Common word-final consonants are voiceless stops and [n s r]. Approximately

Table 2-1. Selected Early Milestones in the Development of Phonology

Age (in months)	Behavior

Phonetic Inventory

Age (in months)	Behavior
1	Produces vegetative sounds (e.g., cough, sneeze, burp).[b]
2-3	Cooing behavior (i.e., sustained production of single vowel sounds such as "oooo" and "aaaah").[c]
	Glottal-velar consonants produced.[c]
3-4	Babbling behavior initiated (i.e., repetition of consonants, vowels).[c]
4	Squeals, growls, raspberries, trills: sounds produced at front of mouth.[b]
6	Begins producing reduplicated babbling.[b]
7-8	Reduplicated babbling.[c]
10	Produces nonreduplicative babbling.[b]
15	Stops and nasals predominate; has approximately 10 segments; syllables consist of simple consonant-vowel sequences (e.g., CV, CVCV, and perhaps VC and CVC).[f]
24	9-10 consonants in initial position, 5-6 consonants in final position.[d]
	Typical inventories: word-initial inventory = [b d g t k m n f s w h], word-final inventory = [p t k n s r].[d]
	Approximately 70% of consonants are correct relative to the adult language.[d]
36	Relative to 24 months: word-initial and word-final inventories are more balanced in size, word-initial [p l j] has emerged, word-final [m n s] has emerged, voiced stops are emerging word-finally, voiceless affricates and consonant clusters are beginning to appear word-initially and word-finally.[e]

Intonation

Age (in months)	Behavior
4	Produces some intonation during sound making.[b]
8-9*	Inaccurately copies intonation patterns.[c]
12	Uses sentence-like intonation patterns.[a]
18-20	Uses jargon.[b]
20-22	Uses questioning intonation.[b]

Communication

Age (in months)	Behavior
3	Vocalizes in response to speech.[b]
3-4	Squeals, grunts, coos, especially when spoken to.[c]
7	Vocalizes upon seeing bottle.[b]
9	Produces "oh-oh" exclamation.[b]
10	Uses ritualized intentional gestures + short sound to obtain desired object.[b]
12-14	Uses voice and gesture to get objects.[b]
14-16	Communicates using gestures, words, and vocalizations.[b]

Age (in months)	Behavior
Communication (continued)	
16–18	Uses words to express wants and to communicate.[b]
20	Child relates experience.[b]
Play	
4	Produces vocal play when playing with toys.[b]
5	Takes turns with sound.[b]
5–6	Enjoys sound-gesture games such as "peek-a-boo."[b]
9–10	Participates in speech routine games such as "pat-a-cake."[c]
12	Produces true words during sound play.[b]
18–20	Uses words when playing by self.[b]
Imitation	
7	May accurately imitate sound sequences (e.g., "oh-oh").[c]
8	Imitates sounds.[a]
9*	Inaccurately copies intonation patterns.[c]
11	Produces and imitates sound and correct number of syllables.[b]
16	Imitates intonation patterns.[a]
16–18	Imitates most words.[b]

Sources: The source for the milestones is the *Kennedy Developmental Scales (KDS)* (Bleile, 1987). The *KDS* is a clinical assessment instrument for measuring the vocal capabilities of children who are developmentally 0–3 years. The *KDS* is a compilation of data from clinical assessment instruments and research studies. For the milestones above, a = the 50–74% attainment criteria in Hedrick, Prather, and Tobin (1984); b = Cassatt–James (1981); c = Saint Christopher's Hospital for Children (1982); d = Stoel–Gammon (1987); e = Dyson (1988); and f = Stoel–Gammon (1985).
* This item appears in both the intonation and imitation sections, because it offers information in both areas.

70% of the consonants are correct relative to adult phonology. By 3 years, the number of consonants in word-initial and word-final positions are approximately equal; voiced stops are emerging word-finally, and voiceless affricates are emerging word-initially and word-finally.

The pitch changes that occur as part of intonation are the melodies of language (Fry, 1982). An early development in the acquisition of intonation occurs near the fourth month when the child produces intonation during sound making. By 8 or 9 months, children produce inaccurate copies of adult intonation patterns, and by 1 year they produce sentence-like intonation patterns. By 18 to 20 months, children often produce sentence-like intonation in long strings, called jargon. By 20 to 22 months, children are able to use questioning intonation as a means of request.

Phonology is primarily concerned with the use of sound for the purposes of communication. One of the early uses of sound for communication occurs near 3 months, when children begin to vocalize in response to speech. Between a child's third and tenth month, the use of sound for communication evolves from squealing and cooing to ritualized gestures and short sounds to obtain desired results. By 14 to 16 months, children usually communicate using gestures, words, and vocalizations. By 16 to 18 months, most children typically use words to communicate. At 20 months, children can use words to relate experiences.

Play may provide a mechanism through which children gain mastery of phonology (Bruner, 1984; Garvey, 1984; Kuczaj, 1983; Weir, 1962). Early vocal play behaviors occur near 4 months of age when children play with toys, and near 5 or 6 months of age, when children begin playing sound-gesture games such as peek-a-boo. At 12 months, children begin using words during sound play, and at 18 to 20 months, they typically use words while playing alone.

Imitation may also provide a means through which aspects of phonology are mastered. An early milestone in the development of imitation occurs near 7 months, when children begin to accurately imitate short sound sequences such as "oh-oh." Imitation continues to evolve until approximately 11 months, when children are able to imitate sounds and the correct number of syllables. At 16 months, children can correctly imitate intonation patterns. By 16 to 18 months, children can imitate most words.

Table 2–2 lists major phonological patterns in the acquisition of English (Ingram, 1974; Shriberg & Kwiatkowski, 1980). As indicated in the Introduction, phonological patterns are descriptions of what children do when they do not produce the correct

Table 2–2. Major Patterns of English

Pattern	Definition
Cluster reduction	Deletion of a consonant in a consonant cluster (e.g., [tu] or [su] for [stu]).
Epenthesis	Insertion of a vowel between consonants in a consonant cluster (e.g., [bəlu] for [blu], [sətip] for [stip]).
Fronting	Substitution of an alveolar stop for a velar or alveo-palatal consonant (e.g., [ti] for [ki], [su] for [ʃu]).
Consonant assimilation	Assimilation of the place of articulation of alveolar stops to the place of articulation of either labial or velar consonants (e.g., [pɪp] for [pɪt], [poʊp] for [doʊp], [gɪg] for [dɪg], [kɪk] for [kɪt]).
Prevocalic voicing	Voicing of a consonant before a vowel (e.g., [doʊ] for [toʊ], [gi] for [ki]).
Stopping	Substitution of a stop for a fricative (e.g., [tun] for [sun], [ɪd] for [ɪz]).
Gliding	Substitution of a glide for a liquid (e.g., [waɪt] for [raɪt], [woʊ] for [loʊ]).
Vocalization	Substitution of a vowel, typically [ʊ]) for syllabic [l] (e.g., [baʃʊ] for [baʃl̩], [dʌbʊ] for [dʌbl̩]).
Reduplication	Replication of a syllable (e.g., [wɑ wɑ] for [wɑtɚ], [kɪ kɪ] for [kɪti]).
Unstressed syllable deletion	Deletion of an unstressed syllable (e.g., [nænə] for [bənænə], [lun] for [bəlun]).
Final consonant deletion	Deletion of a consonant at the end of a syllable or word (e.g., [doʊ] for [doʊm], [pɪteɪl] for [pɪgteɪl]).

sounds and syllables of English. At present, research supports only the most general statements regarding the age range during which these patterns occur in child phonology (Preisser, Hodson, & Paden, 1988).

In general, phonological patterns occur in children between 18 months and approximately 4 years of age. Under 18 months, it is often difficult to discover regular relationships between children's speech and adult phonology. After 4 years, children's errors tend to affect individual sounds rather than sound classes (Haelsig & Madison, 1986). In the author's experience, patterns that are prominent in children under 2 years to 2 years 6 months are Fronting, Prevocalic Voicing, Stopping, Final Consonant Deletion, Gliding, and Reduplication. Patterns that are more prominent in later development include Cluster Reduction and Epenthesis, which occur as consonant clusters begin to emerge between approximately 2 years to 2 years 6 months.

Table 2–3 lists the ages at which children typically produce correct renditions of English consonants and word-initial consonant clusters (Smit, Hand, Frelinger, Bernthal, & Bird, 1990). The earliest age group tested by the study was 3 years. The data in Table 2–3 indicate that sound classes acquired early include nasals, glides, stops, [f], and consonant clusters that contain stops and glides. Various fricatives, affricates, and a range of consonant clusters emerge near 3 years 6 months. Between 4 and 5 years, children acquire additional consonant clusters and fricatives. At approximately 5 years of age, children acquire [θr] and consonant clusters containing three sounds, one of which is a liquid.

Table 2–3. Average Age of Acquisition of Consonants and Word-Initial Consonant Clusters

Sound	Age of Acquisition (years; months)
m n -ŋ h- w- j- f p t k b d g tw- kw-	3;0
v s z- ʃ -ɚ tʃ dʒ r l- sp- st- sk- sm- sn- sw- skw- pl- bl- gl- fl- br- tr- dr- kr- fr-	3;6
-z pr- sl- kl- pr-	4;0
θ ð- -l gr-	4;6
θr- spr- str- spl-	5;0

Source: These data come from Smit et al. (1990). For present purposes, to be considered acquired a sound needed to meet two criteria: (1) at least 50% or more of the subjects — either male or female — correctly produced the sound and (2) no fewer than 50% of the subjects at the subsequent age correctly produced the sound.

CHAPTER 1

Independent Analysis

A variety of approaches are used to study the phonologies of children. Logically, all approaches fall within two categories: either they ignore the adult phonology and analyze the child's phonology as an independent system, or they analyze the child phonology by comparing it to the adult phonology (Stoel–Gammon & Dunn, 1985). This chapter presents problems within the analytical framework of an independent analysis.

An independent analysis typically is used to describe units in the child's phonological system. To illustrate, an independent analysis might describe a child's phonology as containing stops, glides, vowels, and syllables, as well as a co-occurrence restriction that specifies that consonants in a word must agree in place of articulation. Independent analyses do not reveal whether the child's phonology is accurate relative to the adult phonology. For example, it is possible that the child whose phonology was just described pronounced all liquids in the adult phonology as glides. To determine the correctness of the child's phonology relative to the adult phonology requires a relational analysis. In many situations, to gain the fullest picture of a child's phonological development, independent and relational analyses are performed in conjunction.

Independent analyses are particularly useful when analyzing data from children in the earlier stages of phonological development, which typically occur in children under 2 years old. Of course, independent analyses can also be used to describe more developmentally advanced phonologies. This approach, however, becomes cumbersome when describing larger data sets from more developmentally advanced children. When performing independent analyses, especially of children in earlier stages of development, the concept of levels of structure proves a useful notational device.

Independent Analysis Exercises

Exercise 1

The goal of this problem is to provide an opportunity to perform an independent analysis of the phonology of a child under 1 year of age (Ferguson, Peizer, & Weeks, 1973). Investigators have observed that children, especially during the early stages of phonological development, appear to "select" the words they will attempt to pronounce (Ferguson, Peizer, & Weeks, 1987; Schwartz & Leonard, 1982; Schwartz, Leonard, Frome Loeb, & Swanson, 1987). Consideration of the adult words below suggests that some of the characteristics shared by the words include having two syllables, stop consonants, stress on the first syllable, and ending in [i]. An intriguing question is whether the parents choose these words to teach their children, or whether their child chooses to speak only these words. A full discussion of these issues is found in the references cited above.

The problems below are concerned with the child's pronunciation of the adult words. The list of words constitutes the child's entire vocabulary at 0;11.

a.	daddy [dædi]	dædæ
b.	mommy [mami]	mama
c.	doggie [dɔgi]	gaga
d.	?	gægæ
e.	patty (cake) [pæʃi]	bæbæ

1.1 Describe the child's ability to produce words, syllable shapes, stress, syllable types, segments (consonants, vowels), and distinctive features. If there are co-occurrence restrictions, be sure to note them.
(*Hint:* Arrange the data in levels of organization.)

1.2 How could you determine if your analysis describes the real limits on the child's ability to pronounce words?

(*Hint:* Develop a test to determine if the child can pronounce words differently than he or she does in the above five examples.)

Exercise 2

This problem provides another opportunity to perform an independent analysis of a young child. The data are a child's entire lexicon at 1;4 (Branigan, 1976). Focus on the types of syllable and word forms the child is able to produce.

a.	eye	eɪ
b.	goose	gu
c.	hi	ha
d.	bye	ba
e.	kitty	ki
f.	button	bʌ
g.	mouth	maʊ
h.	clock	taʔ
i.	dog	wuwu
j.	daddy	dada
k.	no-no	nunu
l.	popcorn	pap-pap

2.1 What types of syllable shapes, stress patterns, and syllable types can the child produce?

(*Hint:* Analyze the words in terms of stress and syllable shapes, then perform the analysis of syllable types. For example, the word "kitty" has stress on the first syllable and has the syllable shape CVCV. The syllable type analysis for "kitty" is CV.)

syllable shapes:

stress:

syllable types:

2.2 What are the child's two most frequent syllable and word forms?

Exercise 3

The following two problems provide practice in analyzing output patterns. To borrow Menn's (1976) colorful term, output patterns are word recipes. The term "recipe" is intended to convey that children, like some adults who do not spend much time in the kitchen, have a few trusted recipes that they use over and over again.

A number of investigators have studied output patterns, because this phenomenon appears to offer insights into the organization of children's early phonologies (Ingram, 1974; Menn, 1976; Waterson, 1971). In general, output patterns are seldom encountered in normally developing children over 1;8 to 1;10. Perhaps this is because output patterns provide a less successful means for the child to pronounce words as he or she learns more words. Stated simply, as the child's vocabulary increases, his or her speech will become increasingly unintelligible unless output patterns are abandoned in favor of more flexible means of speaking.

The following two output patterns come from a child approximately 1;0 to 1;3 (Menn, 1976).

First Output Pattern
a.   Jacob   dikə / geɪkə
b.   thank you   gædu / dɛtæ

Second Output Pattern
c.   (a)round   da
d.   don't   do
e.   down   dæ / dæn
f.   there   da
g.   toast   doə

3.1 For the first output pattern, describe the phonological characteristics of the child's productions in the following levels of organization: syllable shapes, stress, syllable types, consonant segments, and consonant distinctive features.

3.2 For the second output pattern, describe the limits of the child's ability to produce syllable shapes, consonants, consonant distinctive features, and possible co-occurrence or occurrence restrictions.

Exercise 4

This problem focuses on output patterns in a child approximately 1;6 (Waterson, 1971).

a.	fish	ɪʃ / ʊʃ
b.	brush	bɪʃ
c.	window	ɲeɲe
d.	fetch	ɪʃ
e.	another	ɲaɲa
f.	dish	dɪʃ
g.	finger	ɲeɲe / ɲiɲi
h.	Randell	ɲaɲe
i.	vest	ʊʃ

4.1 Divide the data into two output patterns.
(*Hint:* An output pattern can contain optional consonants, vowels, and syllables.)

4.2 Describe the common characteristics of the output pattern containing the word "fish." Focus your analysis on syllable shapes, stress, syllable types, segments, distinctive features, and possible co-occurrence or occurrence restrictions.

Exercise 5

Finally, this problem offers the opportunity to analyze the phonology of a child approximately 1;10 (Bleile, 1986). This child's speech does not contain output patterns.

Consider the data that follow, then answer the questions below.

5.1   What word-initial consonants (both alone and in clusters) can the child produce? (*Hint:* Organize the results by sound class, placing all stops together, all fricatives together, all consonant clusters together, etc.)

5.2   Not all phonological units in a child's phonology are alike. Some units are infrequent; others widespread and well-established. To derive some measure of how well-established particular consonants are in the child's production vocabulary, determine which of the above consonants occur in three or more different words.

Kylie (1;10)

#	Word	Transcription		#	Word	Transcription
1.	puppy	pʌpi		52.	battery	bʌwi
2.	puzzle	pʌzʊ		53.	bee	bi
3.	pop (n)	pap		54.	boy	bɔɪ
4.	pop (v)	pɑ		55.	blue	bu
5.	pony	poʊni		56.	break	baɪk
6.	pig	pɪg		57.	bread	bʌd
7.	purse	pʊ		58.	brown	bu
8.	pumpkin	pʌmtɪn		59.	dishes	dɪθ
9.	pen	pɛn		60.	duck	dʌk
10.	toy	tɔɪ		61.	daddy	dædi
11.	teddy bear	tɛ.ɪbɛ / tɛtɛ		62.	dad	dæd
12.	turtle	tʊtʊ		63.	dance	dæns
13.	telephone	ɛ.əfoʊn		64.	Donald Duck	dɑnədʌk
14.	tape (n)	teɪp		65.	dinosaur	daɪnəsʊ
15.	tummy	tʌmi		66.	diaper	daɪpə
16.	train	bwaɪn		67.	goat	dɔt
17.	truck	bɑk		68.	game	deɪ
18.	kitty	tɪti		69.	Gumbi	gɑmi
19.	kitty cat	kɪtɪ kæ		70.	grasshopper	gwæsapʊ
20.	cat	tæt		71.	green	gwɪn
21.	cow	taʊ		72.	glasses	bæsəz
22.	Cookie Monster	kʊki mɑsə		73.	monster	mɑsə
23.	Cookie (Mons.)	kʊki		74.	mine	maɪn
24.	cookie	kʊki		75.	meany	mini
25.	Ken	tɛn		76.	mailman	mɛmæn
26.	camel	yamə		77.	mommy	mʌmi
27.	coat	toʊt		78.	momma	mɑmə
28.	comb (n)	toʊm		79.	more	mɔ
29.	crying	baɪ.ɪn		80.	myself	maɪsɛlf
30.	cracker	pʌpə		81.	mouth	maʊ
31.	clown	taʊn		82.	Mickey Mouse	mɪki maʊ
32.	baby	beɪbi		83.	mouse	maʊ
33.	bear	bɛr		84.	Marvin	mɑvɪn
34.	bird	bɔɪt		85.	milk	mɛk
35.	birdie	bʊdi		86.	Mister Brown	misə baʊn
36.	birdies	bʊdɪs		87.	monkey	mʌŋki
37.	ball	bɔ		88.	nose	noʊz
38.	book	bʊk		89.	noisy	noʊzi
39.	bag	bæ		90.	no	noʊ
40.	back (n)	bæk		91.	now	naʊ
41.	butterfly	bʌfəfaɪ		92.	nope	noʊp
42.	bubble	bʌbə		93.	foot	fʊt
43.	bubbles	bʌbəz		94.	fit (v)	fit
44.	banana	bɪnænə		95.	Fuzzy (n)	fʌzi
45.	bananas	bənænəs		96.	frog	fɔg
46.	box	bɑk		97.	front	fʌ
47.	bible	baɪbə		98.	flower	faʊwə
48.	bed	bɛd		99.	sad	sæ
49.	bottle	bɑfʊ		100.	see	si
50.	(baseball)	bat ba		101.	circle	tɪtu
51.	bye	baɪ		102.	supper	dæpʊ
				103.	cereal	sɪwɪ.ʊ

104.	sandwich	sænwıθ	140.	welcome	wɛkəm
105.	sleeping	sipın	141.	wipes (n)	wʌps
106.	slide (n)	baı	142.	one	wʌn
107.	spider	palyə	143.	worm	wʊm
108.	spoon	pun	144.	wet	wɛ
109.	stereo	stɛwə	145.	woopsie	wʊpsi
110.	stuck	tʌk	146.	woops	wʊps
111.	story	tɔwi	147.	yup	yʌp
112.	squeak (n)	bwik	148.	yah	yæ
113.	snack	neık	149.	lion	yaı.ın
114.	sheep	zip	150.	look	yʊk
115.	(grass)hopper	ɑpʊ	151.	rabbit	wæbıt
116.	here	hi	152.	rabbits	bæbıs
117.	hand	hæn	153.	radio	waıyə
118.	hands	hæns	154.	racquet	bæbıt
119.	head	hɛ	155.	Amy	eımi
120.	horsie	hɔsi	156.	airplane	ɛpeın
121.	hurt	hʊ	157.	elephant	ɛfən
122.	hop (v)	ɑp	158.	apple	æpʊ
123.	hammer	hæmə	159.	alright	ɔwaıʔ
124.	hat	æt	160.	off	ɔf
125.	hair	heır	161.	egg	eıg
126.	hi	haı	162.	eggs	ɛgs
127.	heater	i.ə	163.	arm	ɑm
128.	hello	ɛ.oʊ	164.	ok	oʊkeı
129.	vitamin	baı.əmin	165.	up	ʌp
130.	that	dæt	166.	asleep	əzip
131.	this	dıs	167.	Easter Bunny	isə bʌni
132.	there	dɛr	168.	eye	aı
133.	thank you	dæn yʊ	169.	eyes	aıs
134.	thanks	aıs	170.	ears	irz
135.	chicken	tıtın	171.	ice cream	aıs kwim
136.	chickens	kıkınz	172.	owl	aʊwə
137.	chipmunk	tʃimək	173.	owls	aʊwəs
138.	chair	tɛ	174.	awake	əweık
139.	why	waı	175.	oops	ʊps

CHAPTER 2

Relational Analysis

The problems in this chapter provide opportunities to practice the second approach to the analysis of child phonology, relational analysis. This approach entails comparing a child's phonology to the phonology of the adult language.

Exercises 1–7 focus on patterns that are commonly encountered in children's speech. (Table 2–2 lists these patterns.) Being able to readily identify common patterns is important to performing many of the exercises that follow.

The first seven exercises are organized somewhat differently than the other parts of this book. First, the data in Exercises 1–7 are not taken from real children. This approach was taken to simplify the problems. Second, in Exercises 1–3 possible adult pronunciations of the words are given in addition to the child's pronunciations. Third, in the first three problems each word above the rule contains only one pattern. In real children, more than one pattern typically occurs in each word.

Relational Analysis Exercises

Exercise 1

Focus: Word-final consonants

		Adult	Child
a.	dig	dɪg	dɪ
b.	mouse	maʊs	maʊ
c.	bush	bʊ	bʊ
d.	Bill	bɪl	bɪ
e.	bench	bɛntʃ	bɛ
f.	train	treɪn	te
g.	bead	bid	bi
h.	rug	rʌg	wi
i.	fall	fɔl	wɔ
j.	put	pʊt	bʊ

1.1 State in your own words the child's pattern for consonants in word-final position.

1.2 List two words that might be used to determine if the pattern applies to all consonants in word-final position.

(*Hint:* If the pattern applies to all consonants in word-final position, then any word ending in a consonant should undergo the pattern. Stated differently, this question asks you to think of two words that will help determine whether the pattern applies to all consonants in word-final position. For this reason, you should pick words that contain word-final consonants not listed above.)

1.3 This is a common pattern. What is it called?

Exercise 2

Focus: Vowels and consonant clusters

		Adult	Child
a.	block	blɑk	bəlɑk
b.	spine	spaın	səpaın
c.	leapt	lɛpt	lɛpt
d.	skilled	skıld	səkıld
e.	drill	drıl	dərıl
f.	drink	drıŋk	dəwıŋk
g.	spit	spıt	səpıt
h.	cheap	tʃip	tʃip
i.	break	breık	bəweık
j.	drill	drıl	dəwı

2.1 What is your hypothesis regarding the presence of the vowel in the above words?

2.2 If the words in f. through j. were all from one child (they are not) and represented the child's regular patterns, how might you argue that "cheap" indicates that affricates are one unit for this child?

(*Hint:* Affricates might be considered either one or two consonants. The child in this assignment is "made up," but some real children act as though affricates are one consonant. With these thoughts in mind, how does "cheap" indicate that the child believes affricates are one consonant?)

2.3 This is a common pattern. What is it called?

Exercise 3

Focus: Words with three syllables

		Adult	Child
a.	spaghetti	spəgɛʃi	gɛʃi
b.	banana	bənænə	nænə
c.	beginner	bigɪnɚ	gɪnɚ
d.	beginner	bigɪnɚ	gɪnɚ
e.	deliver	dilɪvə	wibə
f.	caravan	kɛrəvæn	gɛwəwæn

3.1 State in your own words your hypothesis regarding this pattern. Be sure your hypothesis is specific enough to account for why "caravan" failed to follow the pattern.

3.2 This is a common pattern. What is it called?

Exercise 4

Focus: Word-final voiced obstruents

a.	bug	bʌk
b.	Dave	deɪf
c.	maze	meɪs
d.	leg	wɛk
e.	of	ʌf
f.	bed	bɛt
g.	bead	bit
h.	big	bɪk
i.	town	taʊn
j.	dim	dɪm

4.1 Describe the pattern in your own words. Why didn't "town" and "Tim" undergo the pattern?

4.2 All of the examples involve consonants at the end of words. Suppose, however, that you found that the child said "pigtail" as [pɪkteɪl]. This word might indicate that the environment for the pattern is syllable-final, not word-final, position. Give two additional words to test the hypothesis that the environment for the pattern is syllable-final position rather than word-final position.

4.3 This is a common pattern. What is it called?

Exercise 5

Focus: Place of articulation of velar consonants

a.	key	ti
b.	go	doʊ
c.	big	bɪk
d.	stick	tɪk
e.	guy	daɪ
f.	coat	toʊt
g.	broken	bwoʊdɪn
h.	digger	dɪdɚ
i.	egg	eɪk
j.	Mike	maɪk

5.1   In your own words, describe the pattern for the place of production of velars.

5.2   Why did "broken" and "digger" undergo the pattern?

5.3   This is a common pattern. What is it called?

Exercise 6

Focus: Place of articulation of alveolar consonants

a.	doe	doʊ
b.	it	ɪt
c.	new	nu
d.	us	ʌt
e.	dot	dɑt
f.	dip	bɪp
g.	mat	mæp
h.	duck	gʌk
i.	good	gʊk
j.	dig	gɪg

6.1   What is your hypothesis regarding the place of articulation of alveolar consonants in the above words?
(*Hint:* Consider a possible co-occurrence restriction.) Give two words to test your hypothesis.

6.2 Two common patterns are depicted in the data. What are they?

Exercise 7

Focus: Manner of production of fricatives and affricates

a.	see	ti
b.	bruise	bwud
c.	bath	bæt
d.	vine	baɪ
e.	you	ju
f.	zoo	du
g.	knife	naɪp
h.	judge	dʌt
i.	we	wi
j.	five	baɪp

7.1 State in your own words your hypothesis regarding the manner of production of fricatives and affricates.

7.2 Give two words that could be used to test your hypothesis. How do you predict the child will say these words?

7.3 This is a common pattern. What is is called?

Exercise 8

The focus of this problem is a relatively uncommon pattern that operates in word-final position. The data come from a child aged approximately 1;9 to 2;2 (Fey & Gandour, 1982).

a.	big	bigŋ
b.	egg	ɛgŋ
c.	read	widṇ
d.	drop	dap
e.	stub	dabm̩
f.	eat	it
g.	word	wʊdṇ
h.	talk	dɔk
i.	lightbulb	jaɪtbabm̩
j.	fit	vɪt

8.1 Describe your hypothesis regarding why the child sometimes added nasal consonants to the end of words.

8.2 Describe in phonetic terms why this pattern might have arisen.

Exercise 9

This problem provides practice in analyzing a relatively uncommon pattern involving vowels and consonants. The pattern is derived from a description of a child aged 1;8 to1;11 (Braine, 1974; Stoel–Gammon, 1983).

a.	ball	bɔʊ
b.	mama	mama
c.	+pad	bæ
d.	big	dɪʔ
e.	+boo	bu
f.	milk	nɪʔ
g.	bʌbʌbʌbi*	babadi
h.	+me	ni
i.	+pa	pa
j.	"B"	dɪʔ

* = a nonsense word that the child imitated

9.1 State your hypothesis regarding this pattern.
(*Hint:* Focus on the relationship between the vowel and the place of articulation of the consonant that precedes it.)
Give two words that would help support your hypothesis.

9.2 Give a phonetic explanation for why this rule might have occurred.

Exercise 10

This pattern is fascinating in its complexity. The data come from a child aged age 1;6 to 2;2 (Cruttenden, 1978). Focus on the assimilation patterns involving place of articulation.

First Pattern
a. doggie   gʊgi
b. cuddle   kʌku

Second Pattern
c. rabbit   babi
d. man   mam

Third Pattern
e. crispies   pipi
f. piggy   pɪpi

Fourth Pattern
g. apple   papa
h. + about   bəbaʊ

Fifth Pattern
i. all gone   gʊgʊn
j. + acorn   kɛkʊn

10.1 Describe the assimilation patterns in your own words.
(*Hint:* Proceed step by step. Try to understand the first pattern, then the second, then the third, and so on.)

10.2 According to your hypotheses, how will the child say "bacon," "a clown," and "sip"?

Exercise 11

This problem focuses on medial consonants. The data come from a child aged 1;11 to 2;1 (Menn, 1971).

a.	daddy	dæ.i
b.	water	ɔ.ɚr
c.	carrot	gæ.ɪt
d.	get it	ge.ɪt
e.	carry	kæ.i
f.	dirty	de.i
g.	Erik's	e.əks

11.1 What is your hypothesis regarding the pattern?
How would the child say "doggie" according to your hypothesis?

11.2 Give two words to test your hypothesis.

Exercise 12

The goal of this problem is to consider the transition between syllables. The data come from a child aged 1;10 to 2;2 (Priestly, 1977). The pattern depicted below is optional.

a.	carrot	kajat
b.	melon	mɛjan
c.	seven	sɛjan
d.	peanut	pijat
e.	panda	pajan
f.	banana	bajan
g.	turkey	tajak
h.	parrot	pajat
i.	berries	bɛjas
j.	lizard	zijan

12.1 What is your hypothesis regarding the pattern?

12.2 Give two words that would either help support or refute your hypothesis. (*Hint:* You might consider testing multi-syllabic words with stress patterns that differ from those in the examples.)

Exercise 13

The following four problems focus on vowels, and, relatedly, on patterns that are optional or have exceptions. The topic of optional patterns and exceptions is introduced here not because vowels contain more optional patterns and exceptions than do consonants, but for two practical reasons. First, vowels are relatively poorly described and thus deserve a little extra consideration here. Second, the concept of optional patterns and exceptions is important for performing the remainder of the exercises in this book, especially those in the next section.

The data for the first of the vowel problems come from a child aged 2;0 to 2;2 (Bleile, 1986).

a.	pig	pʰɪgz / pʰɛgz
b.	pink	pʰiŋk
c.	pen	pʰɛn
d.	pillow	pʰɛwoʊ
e.	tail	tʰeɪ
f.	swing	swɪn / swɛn
g.	hat	hæt
h.	stick	stɛk
i.	fish	fɛs
j.	lip	lɛp

13.1 What is your hypothesis regarding the pattern?
(*Hint:* Focus on vowel height.)

13.2 Is your hypothesis specific enough to exclude all the vowels that didn't undergo the pattern? If your hypothesis does not account for the pattern failing to apply in all cases, you should revise your hypothesis.

Exercise 14

This problem also involves vowel height. The pattern comes from a child approximately 1;6 to 1;9 (Menn, 1976).

a.	tape	ti
b.	duck	dʌ
c.	close	do
d.	okay	ki
e.	gate	gi
f.	whee	i
g.	cow	kaʊ
h.	'A'	i
i.	squish	kix
j.	cake	gik / keɪk

Exceptions to pattern: away, lady, Jacob, rain

14.1 What is your hypothesis regarding this pattern?

14.2 Does your hypothesis account for the fact that some words always undergo the pattern, another word undergoes it optionally, and some words consistently fail to undergo it? If not, you should revise your hypothesis to account for these aspects of the data.

Exercise 15

This problem focuses on the vowel [aɪ]. The data come from a child aged 1;10 to 2;0 (Bleile, 1986).

a.	clown	kaʊn
b.	Danny	daɪni / dæni
c.	flag	fæg / faɪk
d.	bug	bʌg
e.	scared	zɛrd
f.	band-aid	baɪ.eɪd
g.	face	feɪs / faɪ
h.	radio	waɪyə
i.	pig	pɪg
j.	Amy	eɪmi / aɪmi

Exceptions: **The pattern affected approximately one fourth of the words that met its description.**

15.1 What is your hypothesis regarding the pattern?

15.2 Give two words that could help confirm or refute your hypothesis.

Exercise 16

The goal of this problem is to analyze an interaction between vowels and syllables. The data come from a child aged 2;0 to 2;2 (Bleile, 1986).

a.	pole	pʰóʊ.ə
b.	seal	si.ə / siə
c.	pool [pul]	pʰʊ.ə / pʰʊ
d.	grill	gwɪ
e.	(Mr.) Bell	bɛ
f.	full	fʊ
g.	will	wɪ

16.1 What is your hypothesis regarding why the child says certain words sometimes as one syllable and other times as two syllables?
(*Hint:* If you have difficulty with this problem, refer to Table 1–2 on page 6.)

16.2 Using your hypothesis, predict how the child will say the following words: pill, kneel, pull.

CHAPTER 3

Phonological Change

The study of phonological systems undergoing change is one of the most exciting areas of child phonology. From a theoretical perspective, phonological change is intriguing because it often provides insights into children's organization of phonology. For example, at one point in time a child might use alveolar stops where velar stops occur in the adult language. Yet, when the child begins to produce words with velars, the investigator might discover that not all words change. Such a finding might be interpreted to indicate that either the child did not have a single fronting pattern or, for other reasons, some of the words were kept from changing. Regardless of the analysis, such data provide the investigator with insights that cannot easily be obtained by describing the child's phonology from a single time perspective.

From a clinical perspective, phonological change is exciting because it often signifies improvement. For example, in the above illustration, change meant that the child was learning how to pronounce velar consonants. Because change may represent improvement, speech-language pathologists naturally are interested in understanding the cognitive processes that underlie phonological change. The hope is that improved understanding of these processes will lead to better forms of evaluation and treatment.

The exercises that follow offer opportunities to analyze various types of phonological changes. The first assignment shows what might happen when a child attempts new sounds and sound sequences. The second and third problems present data which suggest that change occasionally means the child may temporarily regress in certain phonological skills. The last two problems are relatively open-ended assignments that provide opportunities to describe children's pronunciations of the same word at different points in development.

Phonological Change Exercises

Exercise 1

This problem offers the opportunity to perform a relational analysis of a child learning a new word. The data come from a child named Anthony, who was aged approximately 1;10 at the time of the evaluation (Bleile, 1983). As background, this child had an optional pattern that inserted a nasal stop before a velar consonant, yielding alternations such as [mɪki / miŋki] for "Mickey (Mouse)." The [ŋk] pattern apparently interfered with the child's attempts to learn the name "Ken," yielding the following alternations (one of them quite unkind) in less than an hour.

a. kʰɛŋk
b. kʰaɪn
c. kʰɛn
d. kʰaɪŋk
e. kʰɛm
f. gʌŋk

1.1 Use a relational approach to describe the changes in examples a. through f. (*Hint:* Focus on assimilation patterns.)

1.2 Use your knowledge of phonetics to explain why a velar nasal appears in some of the words.

The next two problems provide practice in analyzing phonological regressions. Phonological regressions involve temporary losses in phonetic accuracy. Such regressions are sometimes believed to arise from the reorganization of the child's phonology.

Exercise 2

The following data come from a child aged 1;6:27 to 1;8:22 (Menn, 1976). The pattern produced an apparent regression in ability. The words involved were "kaka" [kaká] (a Greek word learned from a babysitter that means "feces"), "cookie," and "cracker."

Age (years;months:days)	Words	
	"kaka"	"cracker / cookie"
Before Rule	kaká	káka / kúki
1;6:27	kaká	
1;7:10		kʌkí
1;7:17	gak	
1;7:24	káka	kʌkí
1;7:27	kʌká / káka	kʌkí
1;8:18		kúki
1;8:22	gʌga / kʌka	

2.1 Describe the regression in "cookie" and "cracker." When did it occur? Describe the regression in "kaka." When did it occur?

2.2 Not all English two-syllable words regressed, only "cookie" and "cracker." Menn has argued that the regression involved an output pattern that included the two English words and the Greek word. Looking at the pronunciations in the "prior stage," write an output pattern for syllable shapes and consonants.

Exercise 3

This problem provides another opportunity to analyze a phonological regression. This regression involves word-final consonants. The data come from a child aged 1;10 to 2;0 (Bleile, 1986). In the data below, words affected by the pattern are listed across the top, and the data collection session in which the pronunciation occurred is listed along the left. Sessions occurred every other day.

Session	Words							
	pig	cold	bug	frog	flag	swing	scared	outside
Before	pɪg	—	bʌg	—	faɪk	swiŋg*	skɛd	—
15				fɔgə	fɑgə		stɛd	
16	pɪgə	toʊdə	bʌgə	fɔgə				aʊtsaɪdə
17			bʌg	fɔgə				aʊtsaɪda
18			bʌg	fɔgə		swiŋgə		
After			bʌg	fɔgə	fæg			aʊtsaɪdə

Exceptions: cloud, Big Bird, sad, and dog
* pronounced [swiŋg] by child before rule applied, but pronounced [swiŋ] by parents

3.1 Describe the pattern that led to the regression.

3.2 Develop a phonetic explanation (or more than one: there is no "right" answer to the problem) to explain the pattern.

Exercise 4

This problem and the following one provide opportunities to study the pronunciation of the same word at various ages. The data below come from a child aged 2;2 to 4;0 (Smith, 1973).

Word	Pronunciation	Age
from	1. blʌm	2;7
	2. fʌm	2;10
	3. frʌm	4;0
driving	1. waɪbɪn	2;3
	2. daɪvɪn	2;5
	3. draɪvɪn	2;7
enough	1. nʌp/ ɪnʌp	2;4
	2. ɪnʌp	2;5
	3. ənʌp	2;6
	4. ənʌf	2;8
	5. ɪnʌf	3;0
angry	1. ɛŋi	2;3
	2. æŋgi	2;4
	3. æŋgi/ æŋgli/ æŋgwi	2;5
	4. æŋgi/ æŋgʃi	2;6
	5. æŋgi/ æŋgri	2;7
	6. æŋgli	2;8
	7. æŋgri	2;9
sauce	1. dɔd	2;4
	2. dɔt	2;5
	3. tʰɔt	2;8
	4. tɔt/ tsɔts/ sɔts	2;11
	5. sɔs	3;0

4.1 Use a phonological pattern approach to describe the changes that occurred in the words just listed.

(*Hint:* Some of these changes can be described using the common patterns. Other changes require describing the sounds that changed on a case by case basis. When possible, you should describe less common changes in terms of distinctive features. For example, a change of [oʊ] to [u] might be described as raising of a tense, back, mid vowel to tense, back, and high.)

Exercise 5

This problem also involves analyzing a child's phonology at two ages, 1;10 and 2;0 (Bleile, 1986). The data can be used for a variety of purposes. The assignment that follows focuses on the development of consonant clusters.

KYLIE

		1;10	2;0
1.	puppy	pʌpi	pʌpi
2.	puzzle	pʌzʊ	pʌzʊ
3.	pony	poʊni	poʊni
4.	turtle	tʊtʊ	tɝʃʊ
5.	truck	bʌk	bʌk
6.	kitty	tɪti	tɪʃi
7.	kitty cat	kɪtɪ kæ	tɪ tæ
8.	cow	taʊ	taʊ
9.	Cookie Monster	kʊki masə	tʊʃi manstə
10.	cookie	kʊki	tʊki
11.	Ken	tɛn	tɛn
12.	coat	toʊt	toʊ
13.	crying	baɪ.ɪn	baɪ.ɪn
14.	clown	taʊn	taʊn
15.	baby	beɪbi	beɪbi
16.	bear	bɛr	bɛr
17.	bird	bɔɪt	bʊd
18.	birdie	bʊdi	bʊdi
19.	ball	bɔ	bɔ
20.	book	bʊk	bʊk
21.	back (n)	bæk	bæk
22.	butterfly	bʌʃəfaɪ	bʌʃəfaɪ
23.	bananas	bənænəs	bənænəs
24.	bed	bɛd	bɛd

		1;10	**2;0**
25.	bee	bi	bi
26.	blue	bu	bəlu
27.	break	baɪk	beɪk
28.	bread	bʌd	bwɛ
29.	duck	dʌk	dʌk
30.	daddy	dædi	dædi
31.	green	gwɪn	bin
32.	glasses	bæsəz	dæsɪz
33.	mine	maɪn	maɪn
34.	momma	mɑmɑ	mɑmɑ
35.	more	mɔ	mɔ
36.	mouse	maʊθ	maʊs
37.	milk	mɛk	mɛk
38.	monkey	mʌŋki	mʌŋki
39.	nose	noʊz	noʊz
40.	no	noʊ	noʊ
41.	nope	noʊp	noʊp
42.	foot	fʊt	fʊʔ
43.	frog	fɔg	fɔg
44.	flower	faʊwə	faʊwə
45.	sad	sæ	sæd
46.	circle	tɪtʊ	sɛkʊ
47.	cereal	sɪwɪ.ʊ	sɪwɪ.ɔ
48.	sleeping	sipɪn	tipɪn
49.	slide (n)	baɪ	saɪd
50.	spider	paɪyə	spaɪdə
51.	spoon	pun	spun
52.	snack	neɪk	sneɪk
53.	(grass)hopper	ɑpʊ	hɑpʊ
54.	here	hi	hir
55.	hands	hæns	hænz
56.	hurt	hʊ	hʊt
57.	hair	heɪr	hɛr
58.	this	dɪs	θɪs
59.	thanks	aɪs	dæŋks
60.	chicken	tɪtɪn	tɪkɪn
61.	chickens	kɪkɪnz	tɪkɪns
62.	why	waɪ	waɪ
63.	woops	wʊps	wʊps
64.	yah	yæ	yæ
65.	lion	yaɪ.ɪn	yaɪ.ɪn
66.	rabbit	wæbɪt	wæbɪt
67.	rabbits	bæbɪs	wæbɪs
68.	Amy	eɪmi	eɪmi
69.	airplane	ɛpeɪn	oʊpweɪn
70.	elephant	ɛfən	ɛfɪn
71.	apple	æpʊ	æpʊ
72.	ok	oʊkeɪ	oʊteɪ
73.	eye	aɪ	aɪ
74.	eyes	aɪs	aɪz
75.	ears	irz	ɛrz
76.	ice cream	aɪs kwim	aɪs kwim
77.	owl	aʊwə	aʊwə

5.1 Perform a relational analysis on the development of the child's ability to produce [s] in the beginning of words, both alone and in consonant clusters.

(*Hint:* Ask yourself how the child's ability to produce consonant clusters in word-initial position changes over time.)

CHAPTER 4

Individual Differences

The existence of extensive individual differences is both a problem and a matter of great theoretical interest (Stoel–Gammon & Cooper, 1984; Goad & Ingram, 1987; Macken & Ferguson, 1983; Schwartz, Leonard, Wilcox, & Folger, 1980). Individual differences are a problem because they limit the ability of investigators to reach general conclusions regarding phonological development. For example, because of extensive individual differences, the description of developmental milestones presented in the beginning of Chapter 1 contained a number of caveats regarding the need to remember the differing rates in which children acquire phonology.

As a theoretical issue, individual differences are extremely interesting for at least two reasons. First, individual differences raise the issue of how children who appear to differ so extensively all come to acquire similar variants of the same adult language (Menn, 1976). As a theoretical problem, this means that individual differences present the challenge of developing models of acquisition that are sufficiently flexible to permit individuals to vary on almost all known parameters, yet are also sufficiently constrained to lead learners to the adult phonology. Second, extensive individual differences beg the question of what factors best account for these differences. At present, extensive individual differences appear to result from a combination of factors, including (but probably not limited to) parental teaching style, the child's intelligence and problem-solving skills, the family's social class, and the child's chance exposure to particular phonological units.

The problems in this section focus on data from four children, each approximately 2 years old. The children's names are Hildegard (Leopold, 1947), Kylie (Bleile, 1986), Amahl (Smith, 1973), and Jake (Bleile, 1986). In the interest of readability, the data that follow do not present all of the phonetic details of the children's productions. For complete phonetic interpretations of the transcriptions, the reader is referred to the original sources. For convenience, the phonetic details for the data from Bleile (1986) are listed in Appendix B.

The data can be approached from either the perspective of relational or independent analysis. The first problem focuses on establishing segment inventories, a relatively straightforward form of analysis that serves both to illustrate the extent of the differences between the children and to provide practice in a type of analysis that is widely used in clinical settings. The second problem focuses on comparing the children's segments to normative developmental data.

Hildegard

1.	pillow	bi		53.	boat	bot	
2.	piece	bis		54.	balloon	bu	
3.	peas	bi		55.	broken	bok	
4.	piano	ba		56.	brief (noun)	bitʃ	
5.	papa	baba		57.	blow	bo	
6.	pail	bea		58.	block	bak	
7.	pick	bɪt		59.	down	dɔ	
8.	put	bʊ		60.	dolly	da.i	
9.	paper	bubu		61.	duck	dak	
10.	pudding	bʊ.ɪ		62.	dear	diə	
11.	push	buʃ		63.	door	do	
12.	poor	pu		64.	Dodo	dɔdɔ	
13.	pretty	pɪti		65.	don't	dot	
14.	please	bis		66.	doggie	doti	
15.	towel	daʊ		67.	do	du	
16.	toast	dok		68.	dry	daɪ	
17.	too	du		69.	drink	dɪk	
18.	toothbrush	tuʃbaʃ		70.	dress	daʃ	
19.	too	tu		71.	go	do	
20.	train	te		72.	gone	gɔ	
21.	cover	da		73.	Grandpa	nænæ	
22.	candy	da.i		74.	man	ma	
23.	kiss	dɪ		75.	mine	maɪ	
24.	cold	do		76.	money	maɪ	
25.	comb	do		77.	mama	mama	
26.	coat	dot		78.	much	ma	
27.	cake	gek		79.	mouse	maʊʃ	
28.	coat	nʊk		80.	mouth	maʊʃ	
29.	cookies	tutiʃ		81.	make	mek	
30.	cry	daɪ		82.	me	mi	
31.	crash	daʃ		83.	milk	mik	
32.	cracker	gaga		84.	meat	mit	
33.	buggy	baɪ		85.	Milwaukee	wati	
34.	bike	baɪk		86.	now	na	
35.	bite	baɪt		87.	nice	naɪʃ	
36.	box	bak		88.	night	naɪt	
37.	back	bakə		89.	not	nat	
38.	bottle	bəlu		90.	knee	ni	
39.	ball	baʊ		91.	neck	nɪk	
40.	bell	baʊ		92.	no	nɔ	
41.	bear	bea		93.	naughty	nɔ.i	
42.	baby	bebi		94.	noise	nɔɪs	
43.	bake	bek		95.	New York	nɔjɔk	
44.	bacon	bekə		96.	nose	nos	
45.	bathe	be		97.	new	nu	
46.	big	bi		98.	forgot	dat	
47.	beads	bitʃ		99.	feed	wi	
48.	beach	bitʃ		100.	feet	wit	
49.	boy	bɔɪ		101.	fix	wɪt	
50.	bug	bok		102.	fall	wɔ	
51.	book	bok		103.	fork	wɔk	
52.	boot	bot		104.	fly	waɪ	

105.	flower	waʊ		139.	way	we
106.	Florence	woʃ		140.	where	we
107.	throw	do		141.	wet	wet
108.	through	tu		142.	wait	wet
109.	three	wi		143.	wheel	wi
110.	soap	haʊx		144.	walk	wɔk
111.	sandbox	yɑbɑk		145.	ride	haɪ
112.	slide	yaɪ		146.	room	hu
113.	spoon	bu		147.	write	yaɪ
114.	sticky	titi		148.	right	waɪt
115.	stocking	dadi		149.	read	wi
116.	stick	dɪk		150.	rug	wi
117.	stone	dɔɪʃ		151.	Rita	wiwi
118.	scratch	daʃ		152.	roll	wɔ
119.	shoe	ʒu		153.	light	haɪt
120.	highchair	aɪta		154.	lie	yaɪ
121.	hand	hã		155.	all	ʔa
122.	high	haɪ		156.	on	ʔa
123.	Hildegard	haɪta		157.	alley	ʔa.i
124.	Helen	haya		158.	egg	ʔaɪ
125.	hot	hat		159.	eye	ʔaɪ
126.	hat	hat		160.	I	ʔaɪ
127.	house	haʊs		161.	ironing	ʔaɪni
128.	hair	hea		162.	up	ʔap
129.	here	hɪ		163.	apple	ʔapa
130.	home	hɔ		164.	auto	ʔaʊto
131.	hello	yoyo		165.	out	ʔaʊx
132.	this	dɪt		166.	airplane	ʔɛɪpi
133.	chicken	dɪk		167.	egg	ʔɛk
134.	Joey	do.i		168.	in	ʔnt
135.	juice	du		169.	away	ʔəwe
136.	water	wɑlu		170.	ear	ʔi
137.	wash	wɑʃ		171.	eat	ʔit
138.	watch	wɑʃ		172.	oil	ʔɔɪdo

Kylie

1.	puppy	pʌpi	53.	bee	bi
2.	puzzle	pʌzu	54.	balloon	bəlun
3.	pony	poʊni	55.	balloons	bəlunz
4.	pear	pn	56.	bathroom	bæwum
5.	Teddy (Bear)	tɛdi	57.	bug	bʌg
6.	turtle	tɜ ʃʊ	58.	blue	bəlu
7.	tea	tʰi	59.	break	beɪk
8.	table	teɪbʊ	60.	broken	boʊkɪn
9.	two	toʊ	61.	bread	bwɛ
10.	tired	taɪ.əd	62.	duck	dʌk
11.	too much	tu mʌts	63.	ducks	dʌks
12.	truck	bʌk	64.	daddy	dædi
13.	tractor	bʌtsə	65.	dog	dɔg
14.	tree	bwi	66.	doggie	dɔgi
15.	triangle	baɪ.æŋgʊ	67.	daisy	deɪzi
16.	kitty	tɪʃi	68.	dolly	dɑdi
17.	kitty cat	tɪ tæ	69.	go	doʊ
18.	cow	taʊ	70.	girl	dʊ
19.	Cookie Monster	tuʃi mɑnstə	71.	Grandpa	dæpə
20.	cookie	tʊki	72.	grapes	deɪps
21.	Ken	tɛn	73.	grass	bwæs
22.	coat	toʊ	74.	green	bin
23.	car	tɑ	75.	Grab Bag Party	bɑ bæg paʃi
24.	candy	tæni	76.	glasses	dæsɪz
25.	kiss	tɪs	77.	mine	maɪn
26.	Corrie	tɔwi	78.	me	mi
27.	curtain	tʊ.ɪn	79.	momma	mɑmɑ
28.	carrot	tɛwɪ	80.	more	mɔ
29.	coming (v)	tʌmɪn	81.	mouse	maʊs
30.	keys	tiz	82.	milk	mɛk
31.	cake	teɪk	83.	monkey	mʌŋki
32.	corn	pɔn	84.	messing (v)	mɛsɪn
33.	cards	taɪz	85.	mackerel	mækʊ
34.	crying	baɪ.ɪn	86.	Mark	mʌk
35.	cream	kwim	87.	money	mʌni
36.	clown	taʊn	88.	moon	mun
37.	close	toʊz	89.	music	muzɪk
38.	closed	toʊzd	90.	man	mæn
39.	Cliford	tɪfɔ	91.	mens (pl)	mɛn
40.	quilt	pɪ	92.	moo	mu
41.	queen	bwi	93.	nest	nɛt
42.	baby	beɪbi	94.	nose	noʊz
43.	bear	bɛr	95.	no	noʊ
44.	bird	bʊd	96.	nope	noʊp
45.	birdie	bʊdi	97.	neck	nʌk
46.	ball	bɔ	98.	knee	ni
47.	book	bʊk	99.	knife	naɪf
48.	back (n)	bæk	100.	foot	fʊʔ
49.	butterfly	bʌʃəfaɪ	101.	foots	fʊts
50.	bananas	bənænəs	102.	fish (n)	fɛs
51.	bible class	baɪbə bæs	103.	fun	fʌn
52.	bed	bɛd	104.	first	fʊst

105.	firemen	faɪ.əmɛn	155.	zebra	zɛbə
106.	frog	fɔg	156.	xenophone	zʌdəfoʊn
107.	flower	faʊwə	157.	chicken	tɪkɪn
108.	flowers	faʊwəz	158.	chickens	tɪkɪns
109.	fly (n)	faɪ	159.	cheeks	tiks
110.	sad	fæd	160.	jelly	dɛdi
111.	scissors	sɪzʊs	161.	jumps	dʌmps
112.	sidewalk	saɪwɔk	162.	Jessie	dɛsi
113.	sun	sʌn	163.	jumping bean	dʌpə bin
114.	sunglasses	tunbæsɪs	164.	why	waɪ
115.	circle	sɛkʊ	165.	watch (n)	wɑs
116.	circles	sɛkʊs	166.	walking	wɔkɪn
117.	cereal	sɪwɪ.ə	167.	woops	wʊps
118.	cereals	sɛwəs	168.	yep	yɛp
119.	seal	sid	169.	yah	yæ
120.	Sarah	sɛwə	170.	yogurt	yoʊgʊt
121.	sock	sɑk	171.	lion	yaɪ.ɪn
122.	socks	sɑks	172.	lamby	læmi
123.	Slinky	siŋki	173.	leg	yɛg
124.	sleeping	tipɪn	174.	lawnmower	yæmaʊ
125.	slide (n)	saɪd	175.	robin	wɑbɪn
126.	swimming suit	sumɪn sut	176.	read	wi
127.	sweater	bwɛzə	177.	rabbit	wæbɪt
128.	spider	spaɪdə	178.	rabbits	wæbɪs
129.	spoon	spun	179.	raccoon	wækun
130.	spring	spwiŋ	180.	ring	wiŋ
131.	stars	stɑz	181.	rock (n)	wɑk
132.	stops	stɑps	182.	Amy	eɪmi
133.	stopped	stɑpt	183.	airplane	oʊpweɪn
134.	strawberries	stʌmbɛwiz	184.	elephant	ɛfɪn
135.	scare	stɛ	185.	apple	æpʊ
136.	school	stʊ	186.	alright	ɔwaɪʔ
137.	(ster.)speaker	spik	187.	off	ɔf
138.	snack	sneɪk	188.	ok	oʊteɪ
139.	snow	snoʊ	189.	upside down	ʌpsaɪ daʊn
140.	Snow White	snoʊ waɪt	190.	eye	aɪ
141.	shovel	ʌvʊ	191.	eyes	aɪz
142.	(grass)hopper	hɑpʊ	192.	ear	ir
143.	here	hir	193.	ears	ɛrz
144.	hands	hænz	194.	ice cream	aɪs kwim
145.	hog	hɔg	195.	owl	aʊwə
146.	house	haʊs	196.	on	ɑn
147.	hamster	hæpstə	197.	umbrella	bəbɛwə
148.	hurt	hʊt	198.	again	ədɛn
149.	hair	hɛr	199.	outside	aʊsaɪd
150.	happy	hapi	200.	open	oʊpɪn
151.	highchair	haɪtɛ	201.	opens	oʊpɪnz
152.	hungry	hʌŋgwi	202.	ouch	aʊ
153.	this	ɪs	203.	oops	ʊps
154.	thanks	dæŋks			

Amahl

1.	park	bak	
2.	pedal	pɛgʊ	
3.	peg	pɛk	
4.	pen	bɛn	
5.	penis	bɪnɪn	
6.	pip	bɪp	
7.	play	beɪ	
8.	please	bi	
9.	table	bebʊ	
10.	taking	geɪkɪn	
11.	taxi	gægi	
12.	teeth	tiθ	
13.	telephone	dɛwibu/	
		dɛwibun	
14.	tent	dɛt	
15.	tickle	gɪgʊ	
16.	tie	daɪ	
17.	tiger	gaɪgə	
18.	tongue	gʌŋ	
19.	turn	dʌn	
20.	troddler	lɔlə	
21.	trolly	lɔli	
22.	trowel	daʊ	
23.	truck	gʌk	
24.	cake	gek	
25.	caravan	gæwθwæn/	
		gæwθvæn	
26.	carpet	gabɪ	
27.	cat	mi.aʊ	
28.	coach	guk	
29.	cock	gɔk	
30.	come	gʌm	
31.	come out	gʌmaʊt	
32.	corner	gɔnə	
33.	corridor	gɔɪdɔ	
34.	cupboard	gʌbə	
35.	curtain	gʌgən	
36.	key	gi	
37.	kiss	gɪk	
38.	crib	gɪbə	
39.	crumb	gʌm	
40.	crying	gaɪ.ɪn	
41.	baby	bebi	
42.	back	bɛk	
43.	ball	bɔ	
44.	banana	ban	
45.	bath	bat	
46.	bead	bit/	
		bid	
47.	beetle	bigʊ	
48.	bell	bɛ	
49.	better	bɛdə	
50.	bird	bɪbip
51.	biscuit	bɪgi/
		bɪgɪk
52.	bit (n)	bɪt
53.	bolt	bɔt
54.	book	bʊk
55.	bottle	bɔgʊ
56.	bottom	bɔdɪn
57.	boy	bɔɪ
58.	bump	bʌp
59.	burn	bʌn
60.	bus	bʌt
61.	butterfly	bʌdəwaɪ
62.	black	bæk
63.	blow (v)	bu
64.	broken	bʊgu
65.	briefcase	bik keɪk
66.	brush (n/v)	bʌt
67.	Daddy	dɛdi
68.	dark	gak
69.	ding-dong	gɪŋ gɔŋ
70.	dog(gie)	wowo
71.	door	dɔ
72.	duck	gʌk
73.	drink	gɪk
74.	driving	waɪbɪn
75.	drum	dʌm
76.	dry	daɪ
77.	good	gʊg
78.	glasses	gagi
79.	Granna	læla
80.	grape	geɪp
81.	greedy	gidi
82.	man	mæn/
		mɛn
83.	men	mæn/
		mɛn
84.	mend	mɛn
85.	Mike	maɪk
86.	milk	mɪk
87.	mixer	mɪgə
88.	moon	mu/
		mun
89.	more	mɔ
90.	motorcar	mugəga
91.	mice	maɪt
92.	knee	ni
93.	knife	maɪp
94.	naughty	nɔdi
95.	new	nu
96.	nice	naɪt
97.	nipple	mɪbʊ

98.	noisy	nɔni	150.	hot	ɔt
99.	nose	nu	151.	house	aʊt
100.	now	naʊ	152.	hurt	ʌt
101.	nut	nʌt	153.	there	dɛ
102.	feet	wit	154.	zebra	wibə
103.	finger	wɪŋə	155.	chair	dɛ
104.	fire	wæ	156.	chocolate	gɔgi/
105.	follow	wɔwu			gɔki
106.	foot	wʊt	157.	church	dʌt
107.	fork	wɔk	158.	jam	dɛm
108.	thank you	gɛgu	159.	John	dɔn
109.	soap	up	160.	juice	dut
110.	seat	it	161.	one	wʌn
111.	side	daɪt	162.	wash	wɔt
112.	singing	gɪŋɪn	163.	watch	wɔt
113.	scissors	dɪdə	164.	wet	wɛt
114.	sock	gɔk	165.	wheel	wi
115.	soon	dun	166.	wheelbarrow	wibæwu
116.	soup	up	167.	whistle	wɪbʊ/
117.	sunshine	dʌn daɪn/			wipʊ
		ʌn daɪn	168.	window	wɪnu
118.	slipper	bɪbə	169.	working	wʌgɪn
119.	swing	wɪŋ	170.	workroom	wʌkwʊm
120.	switch	wɪt	171.	urinate	wiwɪ
121.	spanner	bænə	172.	yellow	lɛlʊ
122.	spoon	bun	173.	yes	dɛt
123.	sport	bɔt	174.	ladder	dɛdə
124.	stalk	gɔk	175.	lady	deɪdi
125.	stamp	dæp	176.	ladybird	deɪdibət
126.	stuck	gʌk	177.	lash	dæt
127.	sticky	gɪgi	178.	later	dedə
128.	stop	bɔp/	179.	lawnmower	mɔmə
		dɔp	180.	lazy	deɪdi
129.	struck	gok	181.	leg	gɛk
130.	stroke	gok	182.	leggo	gɛgu
131.	sky	gaɪ	183.	letter	dɛdə
132.	scream	gim	184.	lie (down)	daɪ daʊn
133.	screw	gu	185.	light	daɪt
134.	smell	mɛn	186.	like	gaɪk
135.	Smith	mɪt	187.	little	dɪdi
136.	snake	neɪk	188.	lock	gɔk
137.	sharp	ap	189.	lolly (pop)	ɔli
138.	shirt	dʌt	190.	lorry	lɔli
139.	shoe	du	191.	lotion	dudən
140.	shopping	wɔbɪn	192.	rain	deɪn
141.	shoulder	dudə	193.	red	dɛt
142.	hair	ɛ	194.	ring	giŋ
143.	hammer	ɛmə	195.	Robbie	wɔbi
144.	hand	ɛn	196.	room	wʊm
145.	handle	ɛnu	197.	round	daʊn
146.	hard	at	198.	rubber	bʌbə
147.	head	ɛd	199.	rubberband	bʌbəbæn
148.	hello	ɛlu	200.	running	dʌnɪn
149.	home	um	201.	aeroplane	ɛb ʔeɪn

202.	angry	ɛŋi		210.	eye	aɪ
203.	ant	ɛt		211.	on	ɔn
204.	Adrian	edi		212.	open	ʊbʊ
205.	apple	ɛbʊ		213.	other	ʌdə
206.	away	we/		214.	out	aʊt
		weɪ		215.	outside	aʊtdaɪt
207.	elbow	ɛbu		216.	up	ʌp
208.	empty	ɛbi		217.	uncle	ʌgʊ
209.	escape	gep				

1.	puppy	pʌpi	53.	button	bʌʔn̩
2.	pink	piŋk	54.	bunny	bʌni
3.	purple	pʊpu	55.	bush	bʊs
4.	picture	pɪtʃə	56.	bugs	bʌgs
5.	pig	p°ɪg	57.	bears	bɛz
6.	picnic table	pɪnɪ teɪbu	58.	back (n)	bæk
7.	please	pwiz	59.	bye-bye	baɪ baɪ
8.	plate	pweɪt	60.	bird	bʊd
9.	teddy bear	tɛdi bɛ	61.	birds	bʊdz
10.	teddy (bear)	tɛdi	62.	bicycle	baɪsɪkʊ
11.	tail	teɪ.ə	63.	box	baks
12.	tear	tir	64.	board	bɔd
13.	turtle	tɝ ʃʊ	65.	bananas	bænəs
14.	toes	toʊz	66.	Bert	bʊt
15.	two	tu	67.	break	bweɪk
16.	toothpaste	tupeɪs	68.	brown	bwaʊn
17.	triangle	twaɪ.æŋgʊ	69.	blue	bu
18.	tree	twi	70.	blueberry	bubɛwi
19.	tractor	twækʊ	71.	black	bwæk
20.	trike	twaɪk	72.	blackbirds	bwæk bʊz
21.	twelve	twɛv	73.	duck	dʌk
22.	kitty	kɪʃi	74.	daddy	dædi
23.	cat	kæt	75.	daddy's	dædiz
24.	Cooly (a fish)	koʊwi	76.	Doc	dak
25.	carrot	kɛwɪt	77.	don't	doʊn
26.	Katie	keɪʃi	78.	dark	dak
27.	cookie	kʊki	79.	Do Jo (a fish)	dʒoʊ dʒoʊ
28.	cookies	kʊkis	80.	dandelion	dændiwaɪ.ɪn
29.	Curious George	kɪwi.əs dʒɔ	81.	drink	dwiŋk
30.	cows	kaʊz	82.	drive	dwaɪv
31.	cards	kɑz	83.	goat	goʊt
32.	Ken	kɛn	84.	gopher	goʊfʊ
33.	kangaroo	kæŋgəwu	85.	green	gwin
34.	kangaroos	kændəwus	86.	grandpa	gwæmpɑ
35.	cup	kʌp	87.	grapes	gweɪps
36.	Cristopher	kwɪstəfu	88.	grass	gwæs
37.	cry	kwaɪ	89.	moon	mun
38.	cross (n)	kwɔs	90.	man	mæn
39.	crab (n)	kwæb	91.	milk	mɛk
40.	close	kwoʊz	92.	monkey	mʌŋki
41.	closet	kwɑziʔ	93.	monkeys	mʌŋkiz
42.	clown	kaʊn	94.	motorcycle	moʊʃəsaɪkʊ
43.	book	bʊk	95.	music	myuzɪk
44.	ball	bɔ	96.	Mr. Kennedy's	mɪstə kɛniz
45.	balls	bɔz	97.	mommy's	mɑmiz
46.	bounce	baʊns	98.	move	muv
47.	bubbles	bʌbʊs	99.	messy	mɛsi
48.	birthday	bʊfdeɪ	100.	Mickey Mouse	mɪki maʊs
49.	birthday cake	bʊfdeɪ keɪk	101.	Michael	maɪkʊ
50.	boots	bus	102.	Nancy	nætsi
51.	baby	beɪbi	103.	Neons (fish)	ni.ɑnz
52.	Buster (a toy)	bʌstə	104.	neat	nit

105.	nose	noʊz	159.	heavy	hɛvi
106.	newts	nuts	160.	Herky	hɜ ki
107.	no	noʊ	161.	hand	hæn
108.	nah ([næ])	næ	162.	hands	hænz
109.	football	fɔbɔ	163.	here	hɛ.ə
110.	fit	fɪt	164.	hay	heɪ
111.	five	faɪv	165.	him	hɪm
112.	full	fʊ	166.	hungry	hʌŋgwi
113.	fish	fɛs	167.	hi	haɪ
114.	fine	faɪn	168.	that	dæt
115.	fast	fæ	169.	these	diz
116.	face	feɪs	170.	there	dɛ
117.	food	fud	171.	zoo keeper	zu kipə
118.	front	fwʌnt	172.	chicken	tʃɪkɪn
119.	frog	fwɔg	173.	Jake	dʒeɪk
120.	friends	fwɛnz	174.	Jake's	dʒeɪks
121.	flower	faʊwə	175.	juice	dʒus
122.	thank you	sæŋ ku	176.	Jazzie (a cat)	dæzi
123.	three	fwi	177.	Jazz(ie)	dæzi
124.	sour	saʊwə	178.	yellow	yɛdoʊ
125.	sit	sɪt	179.	huge	yus
126.	set	sɛt	180.	yes	yɛs
127.	sunglasses	sʌŋgwæsɪz	181.	yeah ([yeɪ])	yeɪ
128.	circus	sɜ kəs	182.	yah ([ya])	yæ
129.	seal	si.ə	183.	yep ([ynp])	yɛp
130.	seals	si.əz	184.	one	wʌn
131.	sea	si	185.	walrus	wɔwəs
132.	circle	sɜ̂kʊ	186.	whistle	wɪsʊ
133.	sleeping	sipi	187.	watch (n)	wats
134.	slept	swɛpt	188.	white	waɪt
135.	swing (v)	swiŋ	189.	water	waʃə
136.	swimming	swɪmɪn	190.	woop	wʊp
137.	sweater	tɛwə	191.	woops	wʊps
138.	spoon	spun	192.	writing	waɪʃɪn
139.	star	sta	193.	red	wɛd
140.	stars	stads	194.	room	wum
141.	sticker	stɪkʊ	195.	ready	wɛdi
142.	stuck	stʌk	196.	rock	wak
143.	steps	stɛps	197.	rocks	waks
144.	string	stwiŋ	198.	ribbon	wɪbɪn
145.	strawberries	stwɔbnwiz	199.	light (n)	waɪt
146.	stretch	stwɛtʃ	200.	lion	waɪ.ɪn
147.	square	skwɛ	201.	lotion	woʊsɪn
148.	smile	smaɪ.ə	202.	loose	wus
149.	smash	smæs	203.	apple	æpʊ
150.	snap (v)	snæp	204.	orange (juice)	ɔɪns
151.	snowman	snoʊ mæn	205.	off	ɔf
152.	shout	saʊt	206.	up	ʌp
153.	shovel	ʃʌvu	207.	elephant	ɛ.əfɛnt
154.	shampoo	ʃæmpu	208.	elephants	ɛ.əfɛns
155.	hot	hat	209.	ok	oʊkeɪ
156.	house	haʊs	210.	open	oʊpɪn
157.	Horse Face	hɔs feɪs	211.	ice	aɪs
158.	hoop	hup	212.	Ed	ɛd

213.	elbow	ɛboʊ		218.	orange	ɔɪns
214.	(a)fraid	fweɪd		219.	umbrella	əmbwɛdə
215.	accident	ækɪdɪn		220.	oval	oʊvʊ
216.	albums	æbəms		221.	all gone	ɔ gɑn
217.	excuse me	skuz mi				

Individual Differences Exercises

Exercise 1

The goal of this problem is to perform an independent analysis of the development of consonant clusters.

1.1 Perform an independent analysis of all four children's word-initial consonant clusters. List the children's consonant cluster inventories below.
(*Hint:* An independent analysis does not seek to determine if the consonant clusters are correct relative to the adult phonology.)

Hildegard:

Kylie:

Amahl:

Jake:

1.2 Which child has the most extensive inventory of consonant clusters in word-initial position?
Which child has the least developed consonant cluster inventory in word-initial position?

Exercise 2

This problem provides an opportunity to perform a relational analysis of word-initial consonants. For your own benefit, you should read all the questions before starting the assignment.

2.1 Determine which consonants not occurring in clusters the children can produce correctly in word-initial position.
(*Hint:* Kylie's voiceless stops are all unaspirated, except where noted. Unaspirated voiceless stops would not usually be considered correct in word-initial position.)

Hildegard:

Kylie:

Amahl:

Jake:

2.2 It is important to determine how well-established phonologial units are in children's phonologies. To this purpose, indicate all of the consonants that were correctly produced, those produced correctly in three or more words, and those produced correctly in five or more words.

Hildegard

all:

3 or more:

5 or more:

SECTION II

Phonological Disorders

The concept of phonological disorders encompasses a wide range of disabilities. Some children with phonological disorders have relatively mild problems. For example, a child with a mild disability might be school-aged and have errors in one or two late acquired sounds. Other children have phonological disorders that are more severe. These disorders may be of sufficient severity to interfere with the ease of communication or opportunities for future success. The most severe forms of phonological disability, which typically occur in conjunction with more general medical and developmental problems, may limit the child's ability to use speech as the primary means of communication.

A question of fundamental importance is who determines if an individual has a phonological disorder? To illustrate this problem, the disability of a child in first grade with an "r problem" may appear mild only from the perspective of the school. To the child who is being teased because of his speech, the phonological problem may seem severe (Crowe Hall, 1991; Silverman & Paulus, 1989). Alternately, the child may not be bothered by his speech problem, but his parents might be concerned that his speech affects his friendships with other children or, if not corrected, will limit his future career opportunities.

At a general level, a child is likely to be diagnosed as having a phonological disorder if the following condition is met: the child or persons in the child's social environment believe the child's speech affects his or her present happiness or chances for future happiness. Within this definition, happiness is broadly defined to include social, financial, and developmental aspects of life. The person in the child's social environment who is best trained to make this diagnosis is the speech-language pathologist. When possible, the speech-language pathologist typically makes the diagnosis after speaking with the child and consulting with the child's parents and with other professionals with whom the child comes in contact.

At a practical level, the diagnosis of phonological disorder is achieved through a variety of procedures. Commonly used methods include comparing the child's phonology to normative developmental data or using clinicians' judgments of intelligibility. Both age and developmental level are used as criteria in interpreting the results of the assessment. In addition, the client's prognosis for improvement must also be considered in the diagnostic decision.

The problems in this section address issues that arise after the diagnosis of a phonological disorder has been made. Major topics covered in this section include the phonological basis for selection of therapy goals, the use of phonetics to assist in achieving the goals of therapy, assessment of the child's phonology, and the capacity for the child's phonology to change as the result of remediation. Other topics, such as principles of learning and cognition, although undoubtedly important to understanding phonological disorders, are beyond the domain of the book.

The analytical skills developed in previous sections are the basis for successfully performing the present assignments. In addition, selected problems depend on the information and principles listed in Tables 3–1, 3–2, and 3–3. Table 3–1 lists the ages at which 90% of the children tested in a recent study were found to correctly produce the consonants and word-initial consonant clusters of English (Smit, Hand, Freilinger, Bernthal, & Bird, 1990). Such information is often used both to determine if a child has a phonological disorder and to select therapy goals. Table 3–1 is used in the latter capacity in several exercises in this section.

Table 3-2 lists the relative frequency of English consonants (Sigurd, 1968). Relative frequency has an obvious relationship to intelligibility. Errors involving high frequency sounds are more likely to affect intelligibility than errors involving low frequency sounds (Bernthal & Bankson, 1988). In addition to being a possible criterion for the diagnosis of a phonological disorder, intelligibility also can be used as a criterion for the selection of therapy goals. Unfortunately, many high frequency sounds are acquired relatively late in phonological development. To illustrate, [r] and [s] are both relatively frequent and also relatively late acquisitions. This suggests that sounds likely to be involved in phonological disorders might also have a large impact on intelligibility.

Table 3–1. Age of Mastery of English Consonant and Word-Initial Consonant Clusters

Sound	Age of Acquisition	
	Females	Males
m	3;0	3;0
h w p b	3;0	3;0
n	3;6	3;0
d	3;0	3;6
k f	3;6	3;6
t	4;0	3;6
g	3;6	4;0
y–	4;0	5;0
tw kw	4;0	5;6
ð–	4;6	7;0
l	5;0	6;0
v	5;6	5;6
pl bl kl gl fl	5;6	6;0
tʃ dʒ ʃ	6;0	7;0
θ	6;0	8;0
ŋ s z sp st sk sm sn sw sl skw spl spr str skr	7;0–9;0	7;0–9;0
pr br tr dr kr gr fr r –ə	8;0	8;0
θr	9;0	9;0

Source: Adapted from Smit et al. (1990).

Table 3-2. Relative Frequency of English Segments

Consonants		Vowels	
Segment	Relative Frequency	Segment	Relative Frequency
1. t	6.95	1. ə	11.82
2. r	6.58	2. i	9.29
3. n	6.29	3. e	4.74
4. w	4.52	4. a	4.63
5. s	3.90	5. u	1.91
6. l	3.30	6. æ	1.54
7. d	3.04	7. o	1.54
8. h	2.63	8. ɔ	.64
9. m	2.61		
10. k	2.45		
11. ð	2.25		
12. z	2.00		
13. v	1.88		
14. f	1.70		
15. b	1.63		
16. p	1.61		
17. n	.92		
18. g	.87		
19. ʃ	.72		
20. tʃ	.46		
21. θ	.42		
22. y	.36		
23. ʒ	.03		

Source: Adapted from Sigurd (1968).

Table 3–3 lists selected phonetic environments that may facilitate children's progress in phonological remediation. Investigators have long known that the production of segments is influenced by the phonetic environment in which they occur (Bynon, 1979; Clements & Keyser, 1985; Hooper, 1976). The list in Table 3–3 represents a selective application of these phonetic principles. To illustrate, the production of voiceless stops might be facilitated by training these sounds at the ends of words. Similarly, the production of voicing might best be facilitated in word-initial position or between vowels. The reader should bear in mind, however, that these principles are more in the nature of propensities than iron-clad rules. As such, they provide "first approximations" regarding where to begin teaching. In some cases, a phonetic principle provides insights into the child's phonology, and so comes to serve as the basis of therapy. In other cases, the phonetic principle does not survive the encounter with the child's phonology, and so must be abandoned as a source of insight into the remediation of the child's phonological disorder.

Table 3–3. Selected Phonetic Contexts to Facilitate Phonological Development

Sound Class	Phonetic Context
Syllable	Syllable-final consonants tend to become syllable-initial when the syllable that follows begins with a vowel.
	The production of consonants and vowels tends to be facilitated in stressed syllables.
Voice	Consonants tend to be voiced between vowels.
	Consonants tend to be voiced at the beginning of words.
	Consonants tend to be voiceless at the end of syllables.
Place	Consonants tend to assimilate to the place of articulation of other consonants.
	Production of velar consonants is facilitated in the environment of back vowels.
	Production of alveolar consonants is facilitated in the environment of front vowels.
	Production of velar consonants is facilitated at the end of syllables.
Manner	Fricatives tend to be produced more easily between vowels.
	Consonants are more likely to be nasalized in the environment of low vowels.

CHAPTER 5

Assessment

The skills needed to perform assessments of children with phonological disorders are similar to those introduced in previous sections. These skills include knowing how to develop and test phonological hypotheses and the ability to reformulate hypotheses in response to new discoveries. Many of the phenomena of interest in disordered and normal phonological development are also similar. Selectivity, output patterns, exceptions and optional patterns, phonological change, and individual differences are all encountered in phonologies of clients with phonological disorders.

Yet, there are important differences between evaluating a normally developing and a phonologically disordered child. Fundamentally, the goal of an evaluation of a normally developing child typically is to characterize a phenomenon, whereas the goal of assessing a child with a phonological disorder typically is to ameliorate a condition. Because the goal is to assist the child's phonological development, evaluations of phonological disorders focus on aspects of the child's phonological system that can be manipulated through remediation. To illustrate, an evaluation of a client with a phonological disorder undertaken from the perspectives of independent and relational analyses would not be considered complete if it did not also include an assessment of the child's capacity to be stimulated to produce an incorrect sound.

A second obvious difference between the two areas is that the study of phonological disorders is devoted to a different population than the study of normally developing children. In the author's experience, evaluating normally developing children typically is much easier and takes considerably less time than evaluating children with phonological disorders. This is because, in many cases, children with phonological disorders have other problems, large and small, that the clinician cannot and should not ignore. To illustrate, school-age children with mild phonological disorders may have low self-esteem and sometimes may experience anger or embarrassment at being taken out of class to attend speech therapy. These feelings may limit the child's cooperation in the assessment of his or her phonological problem.

Children with moderate and severe phonological disorders may have the same psychological reactions as children with milder disorders. In addition, children with more severe phonological problems may also have medical and developmental difficulties of which phonology is only one component. Phonological disorders are relatively common among children with mental retardation, cerebral palsy, language delay, learning disability, hearing impairment, and cleft palate (Blackstone & Painter, 1985). These conditions may limit the child's ability to cooperate with the evaluator.

This discussion is not intended to suggest that evaluating the phonologies of normally developing and phonologically disordered children are entirely different enterprises, nor that children with phonological disorders are either maladjusted or unpleasant to work with. Instead, the intention is to suggest that the evaluation of phonologically disordered children requires additional skills and knowledge beyond those required to analyze the phonologies of normally developing children. The exercises that follow provide opportunities to practice skills introduced in previous chapters, as well as opportunities to acquire new skills.

Assessment Exercises

Exercise 1

The goal of this problem is to perform a relational analysis on a child with a repaired cleft palate. The data come from a child named Tim, who was aged approximately 5;0 at the time of the evaluation (Hodson, Chin, Redmond, & Simpson, 1983). Tim was born with an isolated cleft palate extending posterior to the incisive foramen. A Wardill Push Back procedure was performed to close the cleft at 1;11. In the years following the surgery, Tim experienced recurrent otitis media that required nine pressure equalization tube insertions. An audiological examination indicated a mild conductive hearing loss in one ear and a moderate conductive loss in the other.

a.	basket	bædɛʔ
b.	cowboy hat	aʊbɔɪ hæʔ
c.	black	bæʔ
d.	fork	ɔɪʔ
e.	glasses	dæ.ʌt
f.	horse	hɔɪt
g.	leaf	nip
h.	snake	neɪʔ
i.	soap	oʊp
j.	that	dæʔ
k.	truck	ʌ
l.	vase	beɪt

1.1 Describe the child's pattern for realizing word-final voiceless stops. If apparent exceptions to the pattern exist, be sure to list them.

1.2 In general, why might a child with an unrepaired cleft palate have difficulty producing stops, fricatives, and affricates?
(*Hint:* Use your knowledge of phonetics to answer this question.)

Exercise 2

This problem uses a relational perspective to analyze the phonology of a child with Down syndrome. The data come from a child named Maury, who was aged approximately 5;6 at the time of the evaluation (Stoel–Gammon, 1980). At the time of the assessment, Maury was classified as having a mild deficit in adaptive behavior. His mean length of utterance was measured at 1.92. Maury had been raised in the home and had no history of seizures within a two-year period prior to the investigation.

a.	frog	fɔkʰ / fwɔʔ / fwɔg
b.	bag	bæk
c.	big	bɪg
d.	hug	hʌk
e.	rug	wʌgə

2.1 Describe the various ways Maury realizes word-final [g].
(*Hint:* Your description may have to refer to specific words.)

2.2 Use the age of acquisition data in Table 3–1 to determine whether Maury produces [g] at the age at which that consonant is mastered by 90% of children.

Exercise 3

The goal of this problem is to offer an opportunity to perform a relational analysis of a fairly unusual pattern. The data come from a child named Nora, who was approximately 6;9 at the time of the evaluation (Fey & Stalker, 1986). Nora had a severe language disorder. An oral peripheral examination indicated no anatomical factors that would hinder her from reaching articulatory targets. In non-speech tasks, however, Nora's ability to move her tongue on command was reported to be marked by groping behaviors, and her attempts to repeat [pʌtʌkʌ] were reported to be slow. As the authors observed, the above constellation of characteristics is often associated with a syndrome called verbal apraxia.

In addition to offering a complex phonological problem, this assignment provides the first opportunity to develop an elicitation task. The ability to develop flexible procedures to elicit speech is important because some children with phonological disorders require flexible testing to complete the evaluation. Using a variety of procedures to elicit data also often provides more insights than reliance on only one type of procedure.

This assignment asks you to develop a detailed description of a conversational task. Conversational tasks typically ask the child to relate a story or event or simply to engage in spontaneous speech.

a.	already	əwɛ̃hĩ
b.	any	ɛhi
c.	baby	bɛhi
d.	lucky	lɛhi
e.	other	ʌ̃hɚ
f.	button	bʌhiŋ
g.	color	kʊhi
h.	seven	sɛhin
i.	tiger	taɪhʊ
j.	Betina	bətihə

Note: Not all of the child's words followed this pattern.

3.1 Describe the [h] pattern.

(*Hint:* Your description should specify the phonetic environment where the [h] pattern occurs.)

3.2 Develop a conversation task to elicit more data to determine if your hypothesis is correct.

(*Hint:* Your description should be sufficiently specific that you could enter a therapy room, employ your task, and elicit more data from the child.)

Exercise 4

This problem provides practice in performing a relational analysis of a child with Down syndrome. The data come from a child named Jody, aged approximately 5;4 at the time of the evaluation (Stoel–Gammon, 1983). Jody was mildly retarded, and her speech consisted primarily of single words. Jody's hearing was within normal limits.

A question below asks you to develop a word-level elicitation task. Typically, word-level tasks involve asking the child to identify pictures, complete sentences, or name objects.

a.	apples	mæpof
b.	scissors	nɪdos
c.	+daddy	næti
d.	rabbit	mapət
e.	+puppy	mʌpi
f.	potatoes	nɛto
g.	baby	mibi

Note: The pattern had exceptions, affecting approximately 50% of the words that met its description.

4.1 Using a phonological patterns approach, describe Jody's word-initial consonants.

4.2 Develop a word-level elicitation procedure to test your hypothesis. Be specific and make sure your procedure is sensitive to the child's cognitive and language level.

Exercise 5

The purpose of this problem is to perform a relational analysis of the phonology of a child who appeared to be developing normally, except for the presence of a phonological disorder. The data come from a child named Joe (Gandour, 1981; Lorentz, 1976). Joe was approximately 4;6 at the time of the evaluation.

One of the questions below asks you to develop a sentence-level task. A possible sentence-level task might be to ask the client to tell "one thing" about a picture or object. A modification of this approach might be to have the clinician begin a sentence which the child completes.

a.	Scott's school	[ks]ott's [ks]ool
b.	scar	[ks]ar
c.	sky	[sk]y
d.	skunk	[ks]unk
e.	scout	[ks]out
f.	skate	[ks]ate
g.	squash	[ks]uash

Note: Lorentz's account gives phonetic transcriptions only for the word-initial clusters.

5.1 Describe the pattern for word-initial [sk] clusters. Which word is a possible exception to the pattern?

5.2 How do you think the child will say [st] clusters? Develop a sentence-level elicitation task to test your hypothesis.

Exercise 6

The goal of the following two problems is to perform independent analyses on children with severe phonological disorders. The data for the first problem come from a child named Mike, who was aged approximately 4;8 at the time of the evaluation (Pollack, 1983). Mike was a Korean child, who was adopted by an American couple when he was 2;2. Cognitive and receptive language testing indicated that he was functioning within normal limits for his age.

One of the questions asks you to develop two procedures to determine if a child is stimulable to produce a sound. To be considered stimulable, a child must be able to produce the sound in some context. The context can be either phonetic (i.e., beginning of a syllable, end of syllable, in isolation, etc.) or through a specific mode of elicitation. The mode of elicitation is often imitation.

Stimulability is important to assess because of its prognostic value. Interestingly, clinicians appear divided regarding how best to interpret the results of stimulability testing. In the author's clinical experience, most clinicians believe that being stimulable indicates that a sound is "ready to change" and, therefore, should be a target for remediation. Other clinicians, however, although agreeing that being stimulable means a sound is "ready to change," argue that the sound may change without therapy and therefore is not a suitable goal for remediation. This is a good topic for classroom discussion.

a.	balls	da
b.	dish	dɪ
c.	fast	dæ
d.	got	da
e.	hat	næ
f.	mask	næ
g.	right	na
h.	stand	dæ
i.	sun	da / dan
j.	tent	dɛ

6.1 Describe the child's ability to produce consonants and vowels, syllables, and words.

6.2 Develop two procedures to determine if the child is stimulable for [s]. One of the procedures should involve delayed imitation.
(*Hint:* For the delayed imitation task, you need to develop a means to place a pause between your production of the sound and the child's production of the sound.)

Exercise 7

This problem offers another opportunity to perform an independent analysis on a child with a severe phonological disorder. The data come from a child whose initials were G.G.. G.G. was between 3;7 and 3;9 during the period of the evaluations (Camarata & Gandour, 1985). G.G.'s medical history was unremarkable, except for intermittent otitis media. His auditory comprehension of language was normal as measured by a variety of instruments. During the period of the investigation, G.G.'s spontaneous speech contained five consonants, [b d g n w], and five vowels, [i u ə o æ].

A problem below asks you to develop an imitation task. Imitation tasks are valuable because they offer a quick and easy assessment procedure. One difficulty with relying too much on imitation is that at times imitation may not reflect the child's spontaneous speech.

a.	tea	di
b.	toe	go
c.	go	go
d.	goose	du
e.	key	di
f.	train	gæŋ
g.	dress	gə
h.	dog	gæ
i.	+clue	du
j.	+cloud	gæ

7.1 Describe the child's production of [d] and [g] in word-initial position. (*Hint:* The alternation between [d] and [g] may involve a co-occurrence restriction.)

7.2 Develop an imitation task to test your hypothesis.

Exercise 8

The goal of this exercise is to perform a relational analysis the phonology of a child with a relatively unusual pattern. The data come from a child identified as T, aged approximately 3;9 at the time of the evaluation (Leonard & Brown, 1984). An audiological evaluation indicated normal hearing, and T's language comprehension skills were judged to be approximately 6 months below age level. T's mean length of utterance (which the investigators noted was of questionable validity due to T's unintelligibility) was measured at 2.18.

One of the questions below asks you to develop a sentence completion task. As the name suggests, sentence completion tasks typically require the child to complete a sentence begun by the adult. Sentence completion tasks are a valuable addition to evaluation, because they provide a means to elicit specific forms without having to rely on imitation.

a.	airplane	ʌpæs
b.	apple	æpəs
c.	bath	bæs
d.	bread	bɛs
e.	cook	kʊs
f.	cup	kʌp
g.	eye	as
h.	Gabe	gap
i.	hand	hæs
j.	home	hom

8.1 Describe the child's pattern for producing word-final segments. List two words that you could use to determine if the pattern applies to segments not tested in a. through j.

8.2 Develop a sentence completion task to determine if T can produce word-final [t] in the words "cat" and "mitt."

Exercise 9

The goal of this problem is to provide practice in performing a relational analysis of sentence-length data. The data are from a child named Matthew, who was aged approximately 3;10 at the time of the evaluation (Elbert, 1983). Matthew gave no indication of intellectual or organic disorders, and his hearing was within normal limits. Matthew scored in the 96th percentile on the Peabody Picture Vocabulary Test (Dunn, 1965).

One of the questions below asks you to judge the child's intelligibility. Intelligibility is often judged on a scale. To illustrate, one end of the scale might be *100 percent intelligible.* A mid-point in the scale might be *can be understood if context is known.* The other end point of the scale might be *unintelligible in all contexts.*

Spontaneous Sample (3;10)

a. aɪ ɛt də do dɛ bɪdʌ
I hate to go there because

b. aɪ õ aɪ du it ɛɪdeɪ
I don't like to read everyday

c. ə dʌɔ bʌʔ aɪ aɪ vʔi bɛə
a dull book I like (?) better

d. wi gaə waʔ bʊt
we got a lot of books

e. ĩ ɪ aɪn nʌ̃ ə dɛn
any kind none of them

f. wi dɪ.ən hæ dæ ɪʔ awɛɪ æ ʔom
we didn't have that it already at home

9.1 Describe how this child realizes adult language syllable-initial liquids.

9.2 What do you judge this child's level of intelligibility to be?
(*Hint:* You need to develop a scale of intelligibility. To determine where the child falls on the scale, read the sentences aloud to a classmate and ask him or her to judge the child's intelligibility.)

Exercise 10

This problem focuses on performing an independent analysis on a child with a severe phonological disorder. The data come from a child named BJ, aged 4;3 (Crary & Hunt, 1983). BJ was judged to have normal hearing and speech mechanisms and to be of normal intelligence.

One of the questions asks you to determine the frequency of occurrence of the omitted consonants. Frequency of occurrence is one means to select a therapy goal. As indicated in the introduction to this section, the reasoning behind the use of relative frequency in assessment is that more frequent sounds have the chief effect on intelligibility, and, therefore, highly frequent sounds are potential candidates for remediation.

a.	ride	aɪ
b.	that	te
c.	mouse	maʊ
d.	home	hom
e.	clown	taʊ
f.	bag	bæ
g.	push	pʊt
h.	bad	bʌd
i.	dish	dɪ

10.1 Describe BJ's ability to produce consonants and syllables.

10.2 Use Table 3–2 (page 77) to determine which of the consonants BJ omits in syllable-final position occurs most frequently in adult English.

Exercise 11

The goal of this assignment is to perform a relational analysis on data from a child named Jennifer (Edwards, 1983). Jennifer was approximately 3;10 at the time of the evaluation. Jennifer exhibited normal intelligence, hearing, and physical development; and except for her phonology, her language development appeared normal.

a.	bird	buːʊd
b.	rabbit	wæbɪt
c.	duck	dʌk
d.	tent	tʰɛt
e.	potty	pʰɑki
f.	button	bʌkɛn
g.	radio	weɪgyoʊ
h.	cradle	kreɪgoʊ
i.	middle	mɪgʊ

Note: The investigator reported exceptions to the above patterns.

11.1 Describe the child's patterns for the place of articulation of intervocalic alveolar consonants.

11.2 Is this pattern common? If not, what pattern is more typical of velars?

Exercise 12

This problem offers the opportunity to perform a relational analysis of a child's phonology at different ages. The data come from a child named Christine, aged 5;2 to 5;11 (Grunwell, 1983). Christine spoke a dialect of British English. The evaluation indicated Christine had no significant hearing problem. Based on the assessments performed, her language comprehension fell within normal limits, and her intelligence was at least average.

		Age		
		5;2	**5;6**	**5;11**
a.	bridge	bwɛd	bwɪd̪	brwɪdʒ
b.	christmas	fɪʔfʊʔ	twɪʔtwə	kwɪməs
c.	clouds	bwaə	kəwaʊd̪	klaʊz
d.	flower	faə	fəʊə	fləʊə
e.	glove	bət	gləɣ̣	gləɣ
f.	queen	kəwi	kwin	kwin
g.	sleeping	wipɪŋ	slipɪ̣ŋ	ṣlipɪn
h.	smoke	moʊ / moʊk	moʊk	smoʊk
i.	spoon	pʰu / pʰun	pun	spun
j.	stamps	samp	damp	ṣtampṣ
k.	string	wɪn	twɪn	swɪŋ
l.	train	weɪn / weɪnt	t̮weɪn	tweɪn

12.1 Describe (in general, without reference to specific words) the patterns affecting liquids in word-initial consonant clusters.

12.2 At what age(s) are word-initial C + liquid consonant clusters typically acquired? At what age are they mastered by 90% of children?
(*Hint:* Use Tables 2–3 and 3–3 on pages 23 and 78 to answer these questions.)

Exercise 13

This problem offers an opportunity to perform an independent analysis. In contrast to past exercises, the goal is to solve the problem as quickly as possible. This goal is important when, as a clinician, you do not want to perform an in-depth phonological analysis. This situation often occurs when the client appears to have a mild phonological problem or when phonology is not the principle goal of therapy. In both situations, the clinician may want only sufficient information to guide the selection of words to teach the child. This requires a quick assessment of the client's best-established segments, syllables, words, stress shapes, and possible co-occurrence restrictions.

13.1 Make a tentative hypothesis regarding the data described in Independent Analysis Exercise 5 on page 30. Based on your analysis, list three words that fit the child's pattern.
(*Hint:* First, spend a minute studying the data. Next, hazard some educated guesses regarding the child's best established segments, syllables, words, and stress pattern(s). If you notice any co-occurrence restrictions, note them.)

13.2 Perform the same analysis for Kylie at 24 months.

(*Hint:* Remember, you are not being asked to perform an in-depth analysis; you only need to provide a first approximation.)

Exercise 14

This problem provides practice in performing a relational analysis to determine the phonetic environment in which the child is best able to produce a sound. This knowledge can be useful in deciding in which environment to begin therapy.

The best environment is determined based on the percentage of correct productions. To illustrate, if a child produced [t] accurately on 30% of the opportunities in syllable-final position and 10% of the total opportunities in syllable-initial position, then the best environment to teach [t] would be in the syllable-final position. Similarly, if a child produced [s] only between vowels, then the best environment for beginning to teach [s] would be between vowels.

For this assignment, return to the data on individual differences in Chapter 4 (pp. 59–62).

14.1 Which is Kylie's best environment for producing [k]?

14.2 Which is Hildegard's best environment for producing [k]?

Exercise 15

Consideration of formal assessment instruments lies beyond the domain of this book. It may be informative, however, to observe how different assessment instruments describe the same phonological patterns. The patterns below were derived from two children. The first child was a 6-year-old girl judged to have a mild articulation problem, and the second child was a 4-year-old boy judged to have a moderate to severe phonological problem. Most investigators would agree that extremely complex phonological patterns lie largely beyond the analytical domain of existing formal instruments. Therefore, the data appearing below have been simplified to some extent.

Pattern 1 (6;0, delayed)

r → w
s → θ
z → ð
ʒ → dʒ

Pattern 2 (4;0, delayed)

Stopping of fricatives
Pre-vocalic voicing
Word-final devoicing
Gliding
Fronting (50% of occurrences)
Weak syllable deletion

15.1 The assignment is to analyze the patterns within the framework of two assessment instruments. For example, it might be interesting to describe the data from both the perspective of a traditional articulation test and a phonological process approach. Alternatively, you could compare two instruments of the same type, such as two articulation tests, two distinctive feature tests, or two phonological process tests.

CHAPTER 6

Remediation

As with the other topics in this book, phonological remediation entails the development and testing of hypotheses. The hypotheses developed in the previous chapter sought to characterize the child's phonology to determine the most expedient method to induce change. In the remediation of phonological disorders, hypotheses focus on how to select, carry out, and re-evaluate therapy goals.

The exercises in this chapter provide opportunities to consider issues in the remediation of phonological disorders. The assignments emphasize developing theoretical bases for therapy decisions and using the knowledge of phonetics to choose therapy goals and carry out plans of remediation. Special attention is given to identifying phonetic contexts that may facilitate remediation efforts.

Remediation Exercises

Exercise 1

This problem offers the opportunity to consider the selection of therapy goals. For this assignment, your client is Nora, the child described in Assessment Exercise 3 on page 82. Suppose your therapy seeks to correct her [h] pattern. Suppose also that Nora's [h] pattern is the most widespread pattern in her phonology.

Therapy goals can be selected based on various criteria. The selection of which criteria to use depends in large measure on the clinician's theoretical orientation. Common selection criteria include:

1. Selection of the sound that is acquired the earliest by most children
2. Selection of the most widespread pattern
3. Selection of the sound the child is able to produce somewhere in his or her phonology
4. Selection of the sound that occurs most frequently in adult English

The questions that follow are not intended to suggest "right" answers. Instead, the goal is to help you discover the rationale behind each of the approaches.

1.1 Why might you start therapy with the most widespread pattern?

1.2 Why might you decide to use an age-of-acquisition criteria to select the first sound to teach Nora?
Which sound would you teach?
(*Hint:* Use Table 2-3 on page 23 to help answer this question.)

1.3 Why might you decide to begin therapy by teaching Nora to produce a sound that she can make elsewhere in her phonology?

1.4 Why might you decide to begin therapy by teaching Nora the sound that is most frequent in adult English?
Which sound is this?
(*Hint:* Review Table 3–2 on page 77.)

1.5 Assume you wish to collect more data on Nora's pattern (e.g., to determine if the pattern applies to all consonants in intervocalic environments), but do not want to postpone the onset of therapy. List two words you could use to test these hypotheses and develop a short, simple procedure to elicit the words during a therapy session.

Exercise 2

This problem offers an opportunity to apply your knowledge of phonetic context to assist your client's phonological development. For this exercise, your client is Joe, the child described in Assessment Exercise 5 on page 84. Your focus of therapy is his [ks] pattern.

The questions that follow ask you to discover phonetic contexts that facilitate phonological improvement. The concept behind this approach is that phonetic context influences the ability of children to produce sounds and sound sequences. The context that best assists the client is determined from the clinician's knowledge of phonetics coupled with trial-and-error exploration with the client.

2.1 The child can produce [s] at the end of a syllable and [k] at the beginning of a syllable. Use this knowledge as the basis of your therapy.
(*Hint:* Develop a task that uses this phonetic knowledge to help your client produce [sk] clusters.)

2.2 You discover during the assessment that Joe has a second cluster pattern. This pattern applies in syllable-final position, turning stop + [s] clusters (as in "kits") into [s] + stop clusters (so that "kits" is pronounced [kɪst]. You also discover that Joe can make [p t k] in syllable-final environments. Which of the voiceless stops would Joe probably find easiest to produce as a stop + [s] cluster? Why?
(*Hint:* Consider both the phonetics of [s] and the other consonants. If you need assistance, review Table 1–1 on page 5.)

Exercise 3

The goal of this and the following problem is to consider criteria for changing levels of task complexity during therapy. For the present assignment, your client is T, the child described in Assessment Exercise 8 on page 87.

As might be expected, complexity can be measured in a number of ways. Types of complexity include social complexity, cognitive complexity, and linguistic complexity. Often, more than one type of complexity must be controlled during therapy.

This problem focuses on task complexity. It is assumed that for most speakers the following list represents levels of task complexity for most sounds.

Most to Least Complex:

storytelling and spontaneous conversation
sentences
phrases
words
nonsense syllables
sounds in isolation

Of course, within each of these levels there are also levels of complexity, but that type of complexity is not the focus of this exercise.

For the assignment that follows, suppose that you have been working on the child's [s] pattern at the word level. On the average, T now correctly produces word-final segments in CVC words 65% of the time. Specifically, word-final [t] is produced correctly 90% of the time. Word-final [d] is produced correctly 60% of the time, and other word-final consonants are produced correctly as little as 5% of the time.

3.1 Would you move to a more complex task for any of the word-final segments? If so, which segments?

3.2 If you move to a more complex task, what would it be?

3.3 Would you move to a less complex task for any of the word-final segments? If so, which ones?

3.4 If you moved to a less complex task, what would it be?

Exercise 4

This problem also provides practice in considering the effects of task complexity. For this assignment, your client is still T, the child you worked with in the previous assignment. You are now working at the sentence level, and T has finally reached the point at which 75% of his responses are correct. You move to primarily short story and conversational tasks. In these tasks, T correctly produces word-final segments approximately 5% of the time.

4.1 Should a change in level be carried out?
If so, what type of task would you move to?

Exercise 5

The goal of this problem is to develop a minimal pairs approach to therapy (Blache, 1982). In essence, a minimal pairs approach forces a child to recognize that he cannot always be understood. This understanding is typically achieved by presenting the child with pictures or objects that the child pronounces as homonyms.

The data come from a boy named Tommy, who had Down syndrome and was approximately 5;0 at the time of the evaluation (Bodine, 1974).

bi	piece
	please
	B
	big
ni	pills
	tree
	knee
	sneakers
	think
da	talk
	Kathy
	coffee
	Jack
	jacket
	that
	chocolate

5.1 Pick a minimal pair and develop a procedure to teach Tommy to distinguish between the pair.

5.2 Which pair did you pick? Why?
(*Hint:* There is no "right" answer to this question. You need only to be able to defend your choice.)

Exercise 6

This problem and the problem that follows provide practice in using independent analyses to help clients learn new words. For this problem, your client is a 3;0 child with the lexicon described in Independent Analysis Exercise 2 on page 27. Your goal is to use your knowledge of the client's phonology to assist in selecting words that he will find relatively easy to produce. Review the data in Independent Analysis Exercise 2 (page 27), and then answer the following questions:

6.1 What syllable shape would you use?

6.2 What syllable type would you use?

6.3 Which vowel(s) and consonant(s) would you use?

Exercise 7

This assignment provides another opportunity to perform an independent analysis to help teach a client new vocabulary. For this assignment, however, the goal is to develop words that extend his phonological abilities. However, because you do not want your client to experience too much failure, the words you pick should not be phonetically too difficult for him.

For this assignment, your subject is Mike, the child described in Assessment Exercise 6 on page 85.

7.1 Which consonant(s) do you choose, and in which environments do you teach them?
(*Hint:* There is no "right" answer, but you need to be able to defend your decisions.)

7.2 List three words that meet your criteria.
(*Hint:* You might begin to answer this question by considering the phonetic contexts listed in Table 3–3 on page 78.)

Exercise 8

The goal of this problem is to provide additional practice in selecting therapy goals. Your client is a 5;0 child with the phonology of Kylie, as described in Chapter 2, Exercise 5 on page 31. You decide to work on word-initial fricatives. Many criteria can be used to decide which fricative to work on first. Use the criteria listed below to make this decision.

8.1 Developmental order:

8.2 Frequency of usage:

8.3 Which of the two criteria do you prefer? Why?
     (*Hint:* There is no "right" answer.)

Exercise 9

This problem and the three following problems offer opportunities to use phonetic contexts to help achieve therapy goals. For this assignment, your client is Jennifer, the child described in Assessment Exercise 11 on page 90. Your therapy focuses on her place of consonant articulation pattern.

9.1 If you are training in a V__V environment, which vowel is most likely to maximize Jennifer's success at producing an alveolar consonant? Why?
(*Hint:* Consider the place of articulation of vowels.)

1.2 List two two-word VCV phrases that contain the vowel you indicated above.

Exercise 10

This problem continues to explore the use of phonetic context to assist clients achieve therapy goals. For this assignment, your client is BJ, the child described in Assessment Exercise 10 on page 89. Your goal is to help the child learn to produce syllables ending in consonants.

10.1 Based on the child's productions, which consonant not included on the list is BJ most likely to produce accurately in word-final position? Why?
(*Hint:* Consider the distinctive features in the consonants that the child can produce.)

10.2 List two words that you could use to test your hypothesis.

Exercise 11

This problem provides another opportunity to use your knowledge of phonetics to assist your client. For this assignment, your client is G.G., the child described in Assessment Exercise 7 on page 86. Your therapy focuses on the child's restriction on consonants.

11.1 In which vocalic environments might it be easiest to improve the child's ability to produce consonants? Why?
(*Hint:* There is more than one possible answer to this question.)

11.2 Develop a therapy task to assist the child in improving his ability to produce consonants.

(*Hint:* This is an open-ended question without any "right" answer.)

Exercise 12

This problem provides a final opportunity to use phonetic context to guide your client's therapy. For this assignment, you have clients with the phonological characteristics listed below.

12.1 The client can produce [s] in word-final position. Use this knowledge to develop a task to teach [s] in word-initial position.

(*Hint:* Develop a phrase-level task.)

12.2 The client can produce [k] between vowels. Use this knowledge to develop a task to teach [k] in word-initial position.

12.3 The client has a Fronting pattern in word-initial position. Which vocalic environment is most likely to be facilitative to producing velars? Why?
(*Hint:* Consider the place of articulation of vowels.)

12.4 The client has a Fronting pattern in word-initial position. If you use a CVC word, which consonants at the end of the word would be most facilitative to producing a velar at the beginning of the word? Why?
(*Hint:* Consider assimilation.)

Exercise 13

This problem offers a final opportunity to consider the selection of therapy goals. For this assignment, your clients are Hildegard and Jake. However, now they are 3;6 instead of 2;0. Your therapy focuses on word-initial fricatives.

To answer the questions below, you should briefly review Individual Differences Exercise 2 on page 70. That assignment focused on various criteria for deciding how well a sound was established in a child's phonology. For the present assignment, use the occurrence of a word-initial fricative in at least three words as a minimum criteria for consideration. Next, determine the percentage of times the child correctly produces the fricative.

13.1 If you begin therapy with Hildegard's best established (but still not always correct) word-initial fricative, which segment do you choose?

13.2 If you begin therapy with Jake's best established (but not always correct) word-initial fricative, which segment do you choose?

Exercise 14

This problem is an open-ended exercise. For the assignment, re-examine the data from either Jake, Amahl, Hildegard, or Kylie, and suppose that the child you choose to study is 4;6 instead of 2;0. Assume that you wish to perform therapy with the child.

14.1 Describe (a) your goal for the semester or quarter and (b) what you will do on the first day of therapy. Your description should focus on developing rationales for your approach.

REFERENCES

Bernthal, J., & Bankson N. (1988). *Articulation and phonological disorders.* Englewood Cliffs, NJ: Prentice-Hall.

Blache, S. (1982). Minimal word-pairs and distinctive feature training. In M. Crary (Ed.), *Phonological intervention: Concepts and procedures.* San Diego: College-Hill Press.

Blackstone, S., & Painter, M. (1985). Speech problems in multihandicapped children. In J. Darby (Ed.), *Speech and language evaluation in neurology: Childhood disorders.* New York: Grune & Stratton.

Bleile, K. (1983). Unpublished paper on the phonology of a 22-month normally developing child.

Bleile, K. (1986). *Regressions in the phonological development of two children.* Unpublished doctoral dissertation, University of Iowa, Iowa City.

Bleile, K. (1987). *The Kennedy Developmental Scales.* Unpublished assessment instrument, The Kennedy Institute for Handicapped Children, Baltimore, MD.

Bleile, K. (1989). A note on vowel patterns in the speech of two children. *Journal of Clinical Linguistics and Phonetics, 3,* 203–212.

Bodine, A. (1974). A phonological analysis of the speech of two mongoloid (Down's syndrome) boys. *Anthropological Linguistics, 16,* 1–24.

Braine, M. (1974). On what might constitute learnable phonology. *Language, 52,* 489–498.

Branigan, G. (1976). Syllabic structure and the acquisition of consonants: The great conspiracy in word formation. *Journal of Psycholinguistic Research, 5,* 117–133.

Bruner, J. (1983). *Child's talk: Learning to use language.* New York: Norton.

Bynon, T. (1979). *Historical linguistics.* New York: Cambridge University Press.

Camarata, S., & Gandour, J. (1985). Rule invention in the acquisition of morphology by a language-impaired child. *Journal of Speech and Hearing Disorders, 50,* 40–45.

Cassatt-James, E. (1981). *The Receptive and Expressive Scale for Infants.* Unpublished assessment instrument, Kennedy Institute for Handicapped Children, Baltimore, MD.

Chomsky, N., & Halle, M. (1968). *The sound pattern of English.* New York: Harper & Row.

Clements, G., & Keyser, S. (1985). *CV phonology: A generative theory of the syllable.* Cambridge, MA: The MIT Press.

Crary, M., & Hunt, T. (1983). CV to CVC: A longitudinal report of a child with open syllables. *Topics in Language Disorders, 3,* 35–44.

Crowe Hall, B. (1991). Attitudes of fourth and sixth graders toward peers with mild articulation disorders. *Language, Speech, and Hearing Services in Schools, 22,* 334–339.

Cruttenden, A. (1978). Assimilation in child language and elsewhere. *Journal of Child Language, 5,* 373–378.

Dunn, L., & Dunn, L. (1981). *Peabody Picture Vocabulary Test — Revised.* Circle Pines, MN: American Guidance Service.

Dyson, A. (1988). Phonetic inventories of 2- and 3-year-old children. *Journal of Speech and Hearing Disorders, 53,* 89–93.

Edwards, M. (1983). Disordered phonological systems: Evidence from a case study. *Topics in Language Disorders, 3,* 51–61.

Elbert, M. (1983). A case study of phonological acquisition. *Topics in Language Disorders, 3,* 1–9.

Elbert, M., Dinnsen, D., & Weismer, G. (1984). Phonological theory and the misarticulating child. Rockville, MD: American Speech-Language-Hearing Association.

Ferguson, C., Peizer, D., & Weeks, T. (1973). Model-and-replica phonological grammar of a child's first words. *Lingua, 31,* 35–65.

Fey, M., & Gandour, J. (1982). Rule discovery in phonological acquisition. *Journal of Child Language, 9,* 71–82.

Fey, M., & Stalker, C. (1986). A hypothesis-testing approach to treatment of a child with an idiosyncratic (morpho)phonological system. *Journal of Speech and Hearing Disorders, 51,* 324–336.

Folkins, J., & Bleile, K. (1990). Taxonomies in biology, phonetics, phonology, and speech motor control. *Journal of Speech and Hearing Disorders, 55,* 596–611.

Fry, D. (1982). *The physics of speech.* New York: Cambridge University Press.

Gandour, J. (1981). The nondeviant nature of deviant phonological systems. *Journal of Communication Disorders, 14,* 11–29.

Garvey, C. (1984). *Children's talk.* Cambridge, MA: Harvard University Press.

Goad, H., & Ingram, D. (1987). Individual variation and its relevance to a theory of phonological acquisition. *Journal of Child Language, 14,* 419–432.

Goldsmith, J. (1976). An overview of autosegmental phonology. *Linguistic Analysis, 2,* 23–68.

Goldsmith, J. (1990). *Autosegmental and metrical phonology.* Cambridge, MA: Basil Blackwell.

Grunwell, P. (1983). Phonological development in phonological disability. *Topics in Language Disorders, 3,* 62–76.

Haelsig, P., & Madison, C. (1986). A study of phonological processes exhibited by 3-, 4-, and 5-year old children. *Language, Speech, and Hearing Services in Schools, 17,* 107–114.

Hedrick, D., Prather, E., & Tobin, A. (1984). *Sequenced inventory of communication development.* Seattle: University of Washington Press.

Hodson, B., Chin, L., Redmond, B., & Simpson, R. (1983). Phonological evaluation and remediation of speech deviations of a child with a repaired cleft palate: A case study. *Journal of Speech and Hearing Disorders, 48,* 93–98.

Hooper, J. (1976). *Introduction to Natural Generative Phonology.* New York: Academic Press.

Ingram, D. (1974). Phonological rules in the speech of young children. *Journal of Child Language, 1,* 49–64.

Jakobson, R., & Halle, M. (1956). *Fundamentals of language.* The Hague, The Netherlands: Mouton.

Kuczaj, S., II. (1983). *Crib speech and language play.* New York: Springer-Verlag.

Ladefoged, P. (1985). *A course in phonetics.* New York: Harcourt Brace Jovanovich.

Leonard, L., & Brown, B. (1984). Nature and boundaries of phonologic categories: A case study of an unusual phonologic pattern in a language-impaired child. *Journal of Speech and Hearing Disorders, 49,* 419–428.

Leopold, W. (1947). *Speech sound development of a bilingual child: A linguist's record. Vol. II. Sound-learning in the first two years.* Evanston, IL: Northwestern University Press.

Locke, J. (1983). *Phonological acquisition and change.* New York: Academic Press.

Locke, J. (1986). The linguistic significance of babbling. In B. Lindblom & R. Zetterstrom (Eds.), *Precursors of early speech.* Southhampton, UK: Camelot Press.

Lorentz, J. (1976). An analysis of some deviant phonological rules of English. In D. Morehead & A. Morehead (Eds.), *Normal and deficient child language.* Baltimore, MD: University Park Press.

Macken, M., & Ferguson, C. (1983). Cognitive aspects of phonological development: Model, evidence, and issues. In K. Nelson (Ed)., *Children's language.* (Vol. 4). Hillsdale, NJ: Lawrence Erlbaum.

McReynolds, L., & Elbert, M. (1984). Phonological processes in articulation intervention. In M. Elbert, D. Dinnsen, & G. Weismer (Eds.), *Phonological theory and the misarticulating Child.* Rockville, MD: American Speech-Language-Hearing Association.

Menn, L. (1976). *Pattern, control and contrast in beginning speech: A case study in the development of word form and word function.* Unpublished doctoral dissertation, University of Illinois, Champaign-Urbana.

Menn, L. (1971). Phonotactic rules in beginning speech. *Lingua, 26,* 225–251.

Oller, D. (1980). The emergence of the sounds of speech in infancy. In G. Yeni–Komshian, J. Kavanagh, & C. Ferguson (Eds.), *Child phonology. Vol. 1: Production.* New York: Academic Press.

Pollack, K. (1983). Individual preferences: Case study of a phonologically delayed child. *Topics in Language Disorders, 3,* 10–23.

Presser, D., Hodson, B., & Paden, E. (1988). Developmental phonology: 18–29 months. *Journal of Speech and Hearing Disorders, 53,* 125–130.

Priestly, T. (1977). One idiosyncratic strategy in the acquisition of phonology. *Journal of Child Language, 4,* 45–65.

Saint Christopher's Hospital for Children. (1982, Jan.–Feb.). An assessment tool: The Infant Scale of Communicative Intent. *Update Pediatrics, 7,* 1–5.

Salus, P., & Salus, M. (1974). Developmental neurophysiology and phonological acquisition. *Language, 50,* 151–160.

Schwartz, R., & Leonard, L. (1982). Do children pick and choose: An examination of phonological selection and avoidance in early lexical acquisition. *Journal of Child Language, 9,* 319–336.

Schwartz, R., Leonard, L., Fromm Loeb, D., & Swanson, L. (1987). Attempted sounds are sometimes not: An expanded view of phonological selection and avoidance. *Journal of Child Language, 14,* 411–418.

Schwartz, R., Leonard, L., Wilcox, M., & Folger, K. (1980). Again and again: Reduplication in child phonology. *Journal of Child Language, 7,* 75–87.

Selkirk, E. (1984).On the major class features and syllable theory. In M. Aronoff & R. Oehrle (Eds.), *Language sound structure: Studies in phonology presented to Morris Halle by his teacher and students.* Cambridge, MA: The MIT Press.

Shriberg, L., & Kwiatkowski, J. (1980). *Natural process analysis.* New York: John Wiley.

Shriberg, L., & Widder, C. (1990). Speech and prosody characteristics of adult with mental retardation. *Journal of Speech and Hearing Research, 33,* 627–653.

Sigurd, B. (1968). Rank-frequency distribution for phonemes. *Phonetica, 18,* 1–15.

Silverman, F., & Paulus, P. (1989). Peer relations to teenagers who substitute /w/ for /r/. *Language, Speech, and Hearing Services in Schools, 20,* 219–221.

Smit, A., Hand, L., Frelinger, J., Bernthal, J., & Byrd, A. (1990). *The Iowa articulation norm project.* Des Moines: University of Iowa.

Smith, N. (1973). *The acquisition of phonology: A case study.* Cambridge, UK: Cambridge University Press.

Stark, R. (1980). Stages of speech development in the first year of life. In G. Yenikomshian, J. Kavanaugh, & C. Ferguson (Eds.), *Child phonology: Production.* New York: Academic Press.

Stoel–Gammon, C. (1980, June). *A longitudinal study of phonological processes in the speech of Down's syndrome children.* Paper presented at the Symposium on Research in Child Language Disorders, Madison, WI.

Stoel–Gamon, C. (1983). Constraints on consonant-vowel sequences in early words. *Journal of Child Language, 10,* 455–458.

Stoel–Gammon, C. (1985). Phonetic inventories, 15–24 months: A longitudinal study. *Journal of Speech and Hearing Research, 28,* 505–512.

Stoel–Gammon, C. (1987). Phonological skills in 2-year-olds. *Language, Speech, and Hearing Services in Schools, 18,* 323–329.

Stoel–Gammon, C., & Cooper, J. (1984). Patterns of early lexical and phonological development. *Journal of Child Language, 11,* 247–271.

Stoel–Gammon, C., & Dunn, C. (1985). *Normal and disordered phonology in children.* Baltimore, MD: University Park Press.

Waterson, N. (1971). Child phonology: A prosodic view. *Journal of Linguistics, 7,* 179–221.

Weir, R. (1962). *Language in the crib.* The Hague, The Netherlands: Mouton.

APPENDIX **A**

Exercise Answers

Much of the pleasure of performing studies of child phonology, whether for research or clinical purposes, is in the consideration of alternative solutions. The following pages provide possible answers to most of the assignments in this book. All answers are intended as suggestions. When an assignment seemed too open-ended to permit an answer, a dash appears next to the assignment number.

Review Exercises

Exercise 1

page 8

1.1 m n ŋ

1.2 oral stops, fricatives, affricates

1.3 p b f v (w)

1.4 i ɪ eɪ ɛ æ

1.5 i ɪ u ʊ

1.6   5 / baɪ

1.7   / / = phonemic
[ ] = phonetic

1.8   a. alveolar and velar voiced oral stops
b. high tense vowels
c. liquids
d. approximants
e. front tense vowels, mid and high
f. mid front vowels
g. voiceless alveolar fricative

1.9   *assimilation* = sounds (often adjacent to each other) become more like each other
anticipatory assimilation = earlier sound in word or phrase anticipates some aspect of later occurring sound
preservatory anticipation = later sound in word or phrase preserves some aspect of earlier sound

1.10   The following sound is dental (anticipatory assimilation).

1.11   The preceding sound is voiceless (preservatory assimilation).

1.12   [p] preserves the place of articulation of [m] and anticipates the voicelessness and lack of nasal coupling of [s].

Exercise 2

page 12

2.1   kʰæt

2.2   θɪn

2.3   yunaɪt

2.4   br̥u

2.5   ɡɪvɪŋ

2.6   fɛŋɡɚneɪl pʰalɪʃ

2.7   sɛntʃɚi

2.8   pʰḷiz

2.9   wɪntɚ

2.10   bitʰw̥in

Exercise 3

page 13

3.1   bʌʔn̩

3.2   yunɪvɚsɪʃi

3.3   sɪŋɫ pʰɚsn̩

3.4   baʃṭ

3.5 beɪkn̩ ŋ eɪgz

3.6 dɪdʒəgoʊ

3.7 sɪʃi

3.8 spæŋgl

3.9 saʊnd n̩ fyʒ i

3.10 wɛr yə goʊɪn

Exercise 4 page 14

4.1

4.2

4.3

4.4

4.5

Chapter 1: Independent Analysis Exercises

Exercise 1 page 26

1.1 syllable shapes: CVCV
stress: first syllable
syllable types: CV

segments:
  C: b d g m
  V: a æ
distinctive features:
  C: voiced oral stops, bilabial nasal
  V: low front or low central
occurrence restrictions: consonants, vowels, and syllable types in words must be
      identical.

1.2 In general, teach the child one or several words, and observe if the child's pro-
      ductions of the words follow the above limits.

Exercise 2   page 27

2.1 syllable shapes: V, CV, CVC, CVCV, CVC CVC
       stress: first syllable
       syllable types: V, CV, CVC

2.2 syllable shapes: CV (6 words), CVCV (3 words)
       syllable types: CV (12), CVC (3), V (1)

Exercise 3   page 28

3.1 syllable shapes: CVCV
       stress: first syllable
       syllable types: CV
       consonant segments: d, g, k, t
       consonant distinctive features: non-labial oral stops

3.2 syllable shapes: CVC, CV
       syllable types: CV, CVC
       consonant segments: d n
       consonant distinctive features: voiced alveolar oral and nasal stops
       occurrence restrictions: first C = d, second C = n

Exercise 4   page 29

4.1 first output pattern: 1, 2, 4, 6, 9
       second output pattern: 3, 5, 7 8

4.2 common characteristics of first output pattern
       syllable shapes:
         common: VC (V = high lax; C = ʃ)
         variable: word-initial C
       stress:
         common: monosyllabic

segments:
    common C: ʃ
    variable C: d
    common V: —
    variable V: ɪ ʊ
distinctive features:
    common consonant features: voiceless palato-alveolar fricative
    variable consonant features: voiced alveolar oral stop
    common vowel features: high and lax
    variable vowel features: front and back
    occurrence restrictions: [i] and [U] alternate in one word ("fish"), [d] appears word initially only in one word ("dish"). Other occurrence restriction may exist, but the data are too restricted to determine this.

Exercise 5

page 30

5.1 p t k b d g m n f s h z tʃ y w bw gw st
5.2 p t k b d   m n f s h   y w

Chapter 2: Relational Analysis Exercises

Exercise 1

page 34

1.1 Consonants are deleted at the end of words / syllables. (The data do not allow the exact environment to be determined.)

1.2 "tame" → [teɪ] "meek" → [mi]

1.3 Final Consonant Deletion

Exercise 2

page 35

2.1 Schwa is inserted between consonants in a cluster at the beginning of a word.

2.2 A schwa is not inserted between [t] and [ʃ].

2.3 Epenthesis

Exercise 3

page 36

3.1 In words with the syllable shape unstress-stress-unstress, the first syllable is deleted.

3.2 Unstressed Syllable Deletion

Exercise 4
page 37

4.1 Obstruents are voiceless at the end of words (or possibly syllables).

4.2 "dogfight" "bloodhound" (The voiced oral stop needs to be followed by a consonant so that it will not become syllable initial through resyllabification.)

4.3 Word Final Devoicing

Exercise 5
page 37

5.1 Velars are pronounced as alveolars at the beginning of syllables.

5.2 The velars are syllable-initial.

5.3 Fronting

Exercise 6
page 38

6.1 Alveolars become bilabial when there is a labial consonant in the word and become velar when there is a velar consonant in the word.
"pit" → [pIp]
"take" → [keIk]

6.2 Consonant Assimilation (Labial Assimilation and Velar Assimilation)

Exercise 7
page 39

7.1 Fricatives and affricates become oral stops with the closest place of articulation.

7.2 "sigh" → [taI]
"miss" → [mIt]

7.3 Stopping

Exercise 8
page 40

8.1 A homeorganic nasal is added after word-final voiced stops.

8.2 As the child is finishing the stop, he is lowering the velum.

Exercise 9

9.1 Word-initial bilabial consonants become alveolar before high front vowels.
"pit" → [dɪ]
"bee" → [di]

9.2 The stop is assimilating to the stop place of articulation closest to the high front (palatal) vowel.

Exercise 10

10.1 *First pattern:* velar assimilation
Second pattern: labial assimilation
Third pattern: velars assimilate to labials
Fourth pattern: In words that begin with vowels, a bilabial is inserted before the first vowel if the first consonant in the adult word is bilabial.
Fifth pattern: In words that begin with vowels, a velar is added before the first vowel if the first consonant in the adult word is velar.

10.2 "bacon" → [beɪbɪn]
"a clown" → [kəkaʊn]
"sip" → [pɪp / fɪp]

Exercise 11

11.1 Consonants between vowels become null.
[dʌ.i]

11.2 "buggy" → [bʌ.i]
"puppy" → [pʌpi]

Exercise 12

12.1 Consonants that occur between syllables become [y].

12.2 "happy" → [hæyi]
"shadow" → [ʃæyoʊ]

Exercise 13

13.1 High front lax vowels become mid front lax; the pattern is optional in "pig" and "swing."

13.2 —

Exercise 14

14.1 Mid front tense vowels become high front tense; the pattern has several exceptions, and is optional for "cake."

14.2 —

Exercise 15
page 47

15.1 [eɪ] and [æ] become [aɪ]; the rule has exceptions and is optional for several words.

15.2 "ate" → [aɪt]
"cat" → [kaɪt]

Exercise 16
page 48

16.1 A schwa is added and the word is resyllabified if it ends in long vowel + [l]; the rule is optional for several words.

16.2 "pill" → [pɪ]
"kneel" → [ni.ə]
"pull" → [pʊ]

Chapter 3: Phonological Change Exercises

Exercise 1
page 50

1.1 a. The first two segments are correct, and the child has added word-final [k] and the preceding nasal has been made homeorganic with [k].
b. The first segment is correct; the vowel is now [aɪ]; and the nasal is alveolar.
c. The word is correct.
d. The first segment is correct; the vowel is [aɪ] and the word-final [k] appears, making the preceding nasal homeorganic.
e. The word is correct, except for the final nasal, which is bilabial.
f. The first segment is voiced; the vowel is neutral; and the word-final [k] appears, making the preceding nasal homeorganic.

1.2 The velar nasal appears to result from the velum being lowered at the onset of the velar oral stop.

Exercise 2

page 51

2.1 Regression in "cracker" and "cookie" involved shift of stress to the second syllable, and occurred on 1;7:10. Regression of "kaka" involved shift of stress to the first syllable, and occurred on 1;7:24.

2.2 CVCV; both consonants are [k].

Exercise 3

page 52

3.1 A schwa was added to words ending in voiced oral stops.

3.2 One possible answer: The schwa is the perceptual result of releasing the stop. This result might be due to the child's imperfect (relative to the adult language) control of voicing on the stop. Minor support for this argument is the pronunciation of "swing," which was pronounced [swiŋ] by the child's family, but as [swiŋg] by Jake. This word may indicate some difficulty controlling timing of the velum in word-final positions).

Exercise 4

page 53

4.1 **from:** (1) [f] is stopped and voiced, [l] replaces [r]; (2) deletion of second segment as part of cluster reduction; (3) correct production.

driving: (1) either gliding of liquid and cluster reduction or coalescence of cluster into [w], stopping of [v]; (2) deletion of [r] in cluster reduction; (3) correct production.

enough: (1) first: weak syllable deletion, stopping, second: stopping; (2) stopping; (3) vowel change (variation in input?), stopping; (4) vowel change (variation in input?); (5) correct production.

angry: (1) [æ] raised to [ɛ], deletion of cluster; (2) deletion of [r] in cluster reduction; (3) first: deletion of [r] in cluster reduction, second: [l] replaces [r] in cluster, third: gliding of liquid in cluster; (4) same as first and third in (3); (5) first: deletion of [r] in cluster reduction, second: correct production; (6) [l] replaces [r] in cluster; (7) correct production.

sauce: (1) stopping and voicing of initial and final [s]; (2) same as (1) for initial [s], stopping of final [s]; (3) stopping of initial and final [s]; (4) first: same as (3), but without aspiration, second: affrication of stops in initial and final position, third: correct production in initial position, affrication in final position; (4) correct production.

Exercise 5

page 54

5.1 At 1;10, Kylie correctly produced [s] in two out of eight words, and at 2;0 she produced [s] correctly in seven out of eight words.

Chapter 4: Individual Differences Exercises

Exercise 1

page 68

1.1 **Hildegard:** none

Kylie: kw bw sp st sn spw

Amahl: none

Jake: pw tw kw bw dw gw fw sw sp st stw skw sm sn

1.2 Most developed: Jake
Least developed: Hildegard, Amahl

Exercise 2

page 70

2.2 **Hildegard**

all:	p	t	b	d	g	m	n	h	w			
3 or more:		t	b	d		m	n	h	w			
5 or more:			b	d		m	n	h	w			

Kylie

all:	t	b	d	m	n	f	s	h	z	w	y	l
3 or more:		b	d	m	n	f	s	h		w	y	
5 or more:		b	d	m	n	f	s	h				

Amahl

all:	p	t	b	d	g	m	n		w	r
3 or more:			b			m	n		w	
5 or more:	p	t	b			m	n		w	

Jake

all:	p	t	k	b	d	g	m	n	f	s	ʃ	h	z	tʃ	dʒ	y	w
3 or more:	p	t	k	b	d		m	n	f	s		h			dʒ	y	w
5 or more:			k	b	d		m	n	f	s		h			dʒ	y	w

2.3 Most to least developed based on the number of consonants: Jake, Kylie, Hildegard, Amahl

Chapter 5: Assessment Exercises

Exercise 1

page 80

1.1 [t,k] → [ʔ] (*exception:* "truck"), [p] → [p]

1.2 Stops, fricatives, and affricates are "pressure consonants." It would be difficult to build up pressure with an unrepaired cleft palate because air would escape into the nose.

Exercise 2

2.1 frog: kʰ / ʔ / g   bag, hug: k   big: g   rug: gə

2.2 [g] was mastered by 90% of the males in the study by 4;0. Maury is not within expected age limits for [g].

Exercise 3

3.1 Consonants become [h] when between vowels in stressed-unstressed sequences.

3.2 Example: Present the child with four sequenced pictures demonstrating how to ride a bike. Ask the child to describe each picture in sequence.

Exercise 4

4.1 Place of articulation of the nasal is determined by place of articulation of the first consonant to follow the vowel, except for "rabbit," which may be the result of an assimilation of place of articulation of the [b]; (6) is not an exception if the pronunciation is assumed to be "tater."

4.2 Example: Have child name objects in response to the question, "What's this?"

Exercise 5

5.1 Consonants in [sk] clusters are transposed. (*Exception:* "sky")

5.2 As [ts]. Example: Present a picture containing many activities and ask child to tell you one thing that is happening in the picture.

Exercise 6

6.1 syllable shapes: CV, CVC
stress: monosyllables
syllable types: CV, CVC
segments
  C: d, n
  V: ɪ, a, ɛ, æ
occurrence restriction on [n]: only sound to occur word-finally, only occurs in one word ("sun")

6.2 Examples:
Imitation: "Say this word after me: [si]."
Delayed imitation: "I'm going to say a word. Then I'm going to ask you to say it. Let's practice. [si]. Now you say it."

Exercise 7

7.1 If vowel is high, initial C is [d].
If vowel is not high, initial C is [g].

7.2 Ask the child to repeat words beginning with oral stops followed by high and non-high vowels.

Exercise 8

8.1 All but labial consonants are [s]; "sip," "pig."

8.2 Using pictures. Adult: "My pet isn't a dog, it's a _____."
"A baseball player catches a ball with a _____."

Exercise 9

9.1 Syllable-initial liquids are realized as null (like, read) and [w] (lot, already).

9.2 The author's impression is that the child is moderately to severely unintelligible.

Exercise 10

10.1 syllable types: CVC, V, CV
consonant segments: m, p, b, t, d, h
occurrence restrictions: only [m t d] can occur word-finally.

10.2 [t] (relative frequency = 6.95)

Exercise 11

11.1 Alveolar consonants become velar consonants.

11.2 No, Fronting appears more common.

Exercise 12

12.1 Deletion, Gliding, Epenthesis

12.2 Typically acquired: 3;6–5;0
Mastered by 90%: 5;6–9;0

Exercise 13 page 92

13.1 The most common syllable shape is CV, where C is a stop and V is a pure vowel. Most words are single syllables; in disyllables, stress is on the first syllable and there is reduplication.

13.2 Kylie's best-established syllable shapes are CV and CVC. Consonants are mostly oral and nasal stops, glides, and some fricatives. Most words are monosyllables and disyllables.

Exercise 14 page 93

14.1 Word-finally

14.2 Word-finally

Exercise 15 page 94

15.1 —

Chapter 6: Remediation Exercises

Exercise 1 page 96

1.1 Most widespread pattern: Changing this pattern would have the greatest effect on the child's phonology.

1.2 Age of acquisition: The earlier acquired sounds may be "easier" for Nora to produce.

1.3 Evidence of correct production elsewhere in the phonology: Nora might find it easier to produce a sound that she already can produce somewhere in her phonology.

1.4 Most frequent sound: More frequent sounds are likely to have the greatest effect on intelligibility.

1.5 Words: "apple," "mommy"; procedures: delayed imitation or picture naming

Exercise 2 page 98

2.1 The general strategy would be to design phrases such as "miss Kim," allowing rules of resyllabification to help the child produce [mi skɪm].

2.2 Probably the [t], because [s] and [t] are homeorganic.

Exercise 3

3.1 Probably [t]

3.2 Example: Short phrase or sentence in response to picture

3.3 Probably [d] and all the other consonants

3.4 Example: Simple CV words or simple syllables

Exercise 4

4.1 Yes; perhaps two-word phrases or relatively phonologically complex single words.

Exercise 5

5.1 Possible answer: "coffee" and "Jack."
General approach: Present picture of man (Jack) and coffee.
Put something child likes on one of the pictures and have child tell you the name of picture, picking up desired picture if the child distinguishes phonologically between words.

5.2 Possible answer: "coffee" and "Jack."
Because both are picturable and the homonym group to which they belong is relatively large.

Exercise 6

6.1 CV

6.2 CV

6.3 Consonants: Probably any stop (oral or nasal) and [h]; vowels: probably [u] or [a].

Exercise 7

7.1 [dɛn] in word-initial position

7.2 "nah" and "den" (if it is not crucial that [n] must be preceded by [a])

Exercise 8

8.1 f

8.2 s

8.3 —

Exercise 9 page 105

9.1 [i], because they are produced closest to the alveolar position

9.2 Possible examples: "icky" [ɪki], "a key" [eɪ ki]

Exercise 10 page 105

10.1 Possible answer: [n], since he already produces [m] (nasal) and [t d] (alveolars)

10.2 "pine," "bone"

Exercise 11 page 106

11.1 Because the child's restriction operates in the environment of high tense vowels and not on mid tense vowels, therapy might begin in the environment of high lax vowels.

11.2 —

Exercise 12 page 107

12.1 General principle: Use a short phrase such as "ice and soda," exploiting the tendency for syllable-final [s] to resyllabify to syllable-initial position when the following syllable begins with a vowel.

12.2 General principle: Exploit tendency for intervocalic consonants to be syllable-initial (e.g., "a key" and "icky" are both pronounced with [k] in syllable-initial position). Gradually increase the length of time between preceding vowel and word-initial [k].

12.3 Back vowels, because they are also velar.

12.4 Probably another velar. Velar harmony is found in the phonologies of many children during early stages of development.

Exercise 13 page 109

13.1 [s]

13.2 [s]

14.1 —

APPENDIX B

Transcription Conventions

Transcriptions of Kylie and Jake's speech on pages 31–21, 61–62, and 66–68 contain the following conventions:

1. Voiced obstruents are partially unvoiced at the ends of syllables.
2. Vowels lengthen in open syllables.
3. Except where indicated by a raised circle, voiceless stops that are obligatorily aspirated in adult English are also aspirated in Jake's speech, but not in Kylie's.
4. Glottal stops often occur before words beginning with vowels.
5. Pauses are indicated by commas.
6. Half circles are used to indicate that adjacent vowels were perceived to occur in the same syllable.
7. In Kylie's speech, [f v] are usually labio-dental, but can also be bilabial.

APPENDIX C

List of Exercises

Chapter 3: Phonological Change

Chapter 4: Individual Differences

Chapter 5: Assessment

Chapter 6: Remediation